India Ebook's

ONE SHOT FOR IGNOU MPSE-008

STATE POLITICS

IN INDIA

M.A. – Political Science
MPS – 2nd Year

JANMEJOY DAS

INDIA EBOOK PRESS

Contents

1. DEVELOPMENT OF STATE POLITICS IN INDIA

Introduction
State Politics: the 1950s–1960s
Rise of Regional Forces and State Politics: the 1970s
State Politics: the 1980s onwards
  - ➤ Assertion of Identities
  - ➤ Impact of Globalisation
  - ➤ Insurgencies and State Politics

1.1: One Shot Concepts

INTRODUCTION

State politics as a specialised field of politics in India developed in the post-independence period. The states of Indian Union assumed the form of distinct identities following their reorganisation in 1956. Prior to their reorganisation, they were placed in four categories—A, B, C and D states. But it was only in the 1960s that the political scientists felt the need to study state politics as a specialised subject. The disquieting developments during the 1950s and 1960s in several states prompted a large number of them to study politics in different states.

In an attempt to place the state politics in India in a perspective, two seminars were held in the USA in 1961 (University of Chicago) and in 1964 (the Massachusetts Institute of Technology) with the initiative of Myron Weiner. The scholars working on nine of the seventeen states in India presented their findings in the latter. The report on the first seminar was published in Asian Survey of June1961. The papers presented in the seminar of 1964 were published in the first book on state politics State Politics in India (1968) edited by Myron Weiner. In the similar vein, Iqbal Narain edited a book State Politics in India (1976) which was the first attempt to cover politics of all states in India including Assam and Jammu and Kashmir. Its predecessor, Weiner's book, did not cover all states.

State politics has undergone significant changes in the post-independence period. It has emerged from the periphery of the national politics to the centre stage in the politics of India. Since the 1990s the states have become partners in the coalition governments at the centre. Earlier they occupied secondary position in relation to the centre in India's politics. Now they are in a position to not only set the agenda for the politics in India but have become partners in the formulation of the state policies. The states participate in the national politics by becoming members of one or the other coalition partners. They represent different regional and social forces.

STATE POLITICS: THE 1950s–1960s Book Q.1

State politics in the *first two decades* after **independence** grew under the influence of centre, which focused on the pursuit of the nation-state building in India. During this period the Nehruvian model of development and the single party dominance of the Congress signified the politics in India. State politics was mainly a replica of the national politics. The central government occupied a dominant position in the Indian political system where the state occupied the secondary place. Under the directive of the centre, the state governments introduced several measures in order to contribute towards nation-building, like land reforms, and community development programmes.

Different factions within the Congress representing sectarian interests in the states were appendages of the faction leaders at the national level. The fact that the dominant party reigned in the centre and several states simultaneously gave the impression that there was a common pattern of politics in the states and centre. The governors, as appointees of the sympathetic governments at the centre, with a few exceptions, remained non-controversial. No doubt, it was a dominant pattern. But along with this, there also emerged dissenting patterns simultaneously within state politics. These developments challenged the dominant pattern of politics: the dominant position of Congress and secondary position of state politics. Within a few years of independence the Naga and Mizo insurgencies started in the North-East India, Plebiscite Front movement started in Jammu and Kashmir, and the demand for reorganisation of states was raised in south India.

Even the parties with different ideological persuasions from that of the Congress played a significant role during this period in the politics of states. The socialists and the Left together in Bihar, Uttar Pradesh, Kerala and West Bengal, Jana Sangha in north Indian States, the Akali Dal in

Punjab mobilised the people on difference issues against the Congress. These developments had set a tone for a pattern of state politics which was to emerge in India in the near future. The dalit movement led by the RPI in Maharashtra and UP, and the Dalit Panther in the Maharashtra, the cow protection movement of the Jana Sangha, RSS and their affiliates in north India; socialist movements for the spread of Hindi language and opposition to the imposition of Hindi language in Tamil Nadu and demand for secession of Madras / Tamil Nadu from India were the early examples of ethnic dimension to the patterns of the state politics. The Congress hegemony was also challenged by conservative parties like Swatantra in Gujarat and Rajasthan. These developments had prompted Selig Harisson to call the 1950s as the "most dangerous decade". This pattern found its expression in the defeat of the Congress in several states in the general election in 1967 and formation of the coalition governments in 1969. It set a new trend in the politics in the states of Union of India.

RISE OF REGIONAL FORCES AND STATE POLITICS: THE 1970s

Book Q.2

Changes in the patterns of state politics during the 1960s-1970s took place in the backdrop of the demise of Jawaharlal Nehru – the **decline of the Congress system** and rise of Indira Gandhi who personalised the Congress and institutions of governance. One of the most significant feature of the state politics between the late 1960s and the 1970s had been the rise of the rural rich or the kulaks especially in the areas which had witnessed the Green Revolution. The most relevant examples are those of Jats in UP, Haryana and Punjab; Yadavs and Kurmies in Bihar and eastern UP; Reddies and Kammas in Andhra Pradesh; Vokkaligas and Lingayats in Karnataka, etc.

Charan Singh formed Bharatiya Kranti Dal with the focus mainly on the agrarian agenda. He provided leadership and forum to a strong section in the state politics in north India for two decades (1967-1987). He, along with the state level leaders in Bihar and Haryana, dominated the politics of north India during this period. In a large number of the states strong regional leaders with formidable social bases among the agrarian classes emerged on the lines of Uttar Pradesh. These leaders and parties focused on the regional issues and demanded revamping the centre-state relations.

Imposition of emergency provided an opportunity to several state and national leaders and parties to come together against the dominant Congress. Regional and national parities formed the Janata Party at the national and state levels, and formed the governments in the centre and the states. The Janata Party-led governments both at the centre and in the states introduced certain measures which had repercussions for the state politics. The appointment of the Mandal Commission and introduction of reservation for the backward classes in Bihar and Uttar Pradesh set the new trends which were significant both for the state and national politics. The leadership of the Congress and Indira Gandhi was challenged by the J P movement and Gujarat agitation in the 1970s. Unable to meet the challenge of the regional forces, J P movement and verdict of Allahabad High Court against Indira Gandhi, the centre to imposed emergency in the country for twenty months (1975-1977). The post-emergency era saw the elevation of the regional leaders like Charan Singh to the national politics. Along with this, state level leaders like Karpoori Thakur in Bihar, Devi Lal in Haryana, Ram Naresh Yadav and later Mulayam Singh Yadav in UP and in several south India states started pushing their programmes in the central politics.

STATE POLITICS:THE 1980s ONWARDS

> ### Assertion of Identities

The developments since the 1980s further contributed to the changing phase of the states politics in India and states' role in the national politics. These developments were – frequency of coalition politics at the national and state levels, globalisation, emergence of yet another generation of leadership, assertion of multiple identities based on ethnicity, i.e., caste (dalits and backward classes), tribe, language; the farmers' movements, insurgency in North-East, Jammu and Kashmir and Punjab, and autonomy movements. Movements of different social groups have come to be known as new social movement. Though these developments were caused primarily as a result of the state policies, yet these were distinct features as compared to the earlier period.

The assertion of the dalits and backward classes in the North in the recent period has only contributed to the politics of similar assertion in the south which took place much earlier. Politicisation of the dalits in north India in the form of the BSP, of the backward classes in the form of various incarnations of Janata Dals in Bihar and Uttar Pradesh, and also the non-party fronts related to various castes as well as the religion further added new dimension to the state politics in India.

The period also witnessed the rise of the rich farmers in the form of BKUs (Bharatiya Kisan Unions) in UP and Punjab, Shetkari Sangathan in Maharashtra, Khedyut Samaj in Gujarat and Karnataka Rajya Ryatha Sangha in Karnataka. These groups also had their earlier incarnation in the 1970s when they were addressed as kulaks in the north as well as the south. But there was difference between the trends of the 1970s and those of the 1980s. While the former as the product of the green revolution and the land reforms mainly sought the share in the political power and favourable terms of trade for agricultural products, the latter focused on the issues related to the market economy. The new social forces raised multiple demands in different states. These demands were reflected in the form of reservation, the creation of the new states and greater allocation of resources from the centre to the states.

> **Impact of Globalisation**

The state politics took a new turn towards the end of the last decade of the twentieth century. Globalisation has weakened the position of the centre on the one hand, and enabled the states to be autonomous players in the national as well as state politics. The Foreign Direct Investment (FDI) did not have an even impact on all states; some states have benefited from it while others lagged. In fact, liberalisation has resulted in competition among states to seek investments. Some observers feel that it has created disparity among the states. Some states have become more advanced while others have become more backward. During the phase of globalisation even the party system has witnessed changes. In most of the states two or more than two parties emerged as principal parties. West Bengal presented an exception where one party remained the dominant force. Even here, it has been able to wield power in collaboration with other like-minded parties in the form of Left Front. State level parties are oriented towards specific regions, religion or caste. The role of political parties is generally focused on electoral mobilisation. But emergence of new social forces like the dalits and OBCs has also added to the non-electoral mobilisation in the state. The latter, however, gets linked to the electoral mobilisation also.

➢ Insurgencies and State Politics

Besides the issues discussed so far in this unit, the insurgency and related issues occupy a central place in the politics of several states especially in North-East India, Jammu and Kashmir and Punjab. These are also related to the self-determination movements. These developments not only impact politics of respective states but also have serious repercussion on national politics of the country. The problems of insurgency are related to the issues of development, inter-ethnic relations and autonomy. While insurgency is directed against the nation-state or its referents, in several instances it gives birth to the ethnic riots and conflict among the ethnic groups. Problems of insurgency is not new to India. As mentioned earlier, India faced such problems immediately after the achievement of Independence like Naga and Mizo insurgency in the North-East India, Plebiscite Front agitation in Jammu and Kashmir, demand for a separate sovereign state for Tamil speaking population in south India, etc.

1.2: IGNOU Book Exercise – Solved

1) What were the dominant features of state politics in India in the first two decades following independence?

Answer by India Ebook: Refer the Marked 1 Shot Concept Above.

2) Why did the Congress system or the dominant party system decline?

Answer by India Ebook: Refer the Marked 1 Shot Concept Above.

3) Explain the impact of identities on the state politics in India.

Answer by India Ebook: Refer the Marked 1 Shot Concept Above.

1.3: IGNOU Past 6 Attempts Question – Solved

Dec 2020: Briefly describe the systemic and post-modernist frameworks to analyse State politics in India.2 Q.1 +

Answer by India Ebook: Almost Same as Q.1 plus Post-Modenist.

June 2021: Discuss the Marxian approach to study state politics. 2 Q.2

Answer by India Ebook: Exact Same as Q.2 of Above.

Introduction
Systemic framework
Marxian Frameworks
> ➤ Classical Marxian framework
> ➤ Neo-Marxian Framework

The Post-Modernist frameworks
Federation-Building Framework
Social Capital Framework
Frameworks to Study Elections

2.1: One Shot Concepts

INTRODUCTION

Development of state politics in India was marked by the emergence of new issues, processes and political forces over more than five decades. These changes gave distinct identity to the state politics. They also drew the attention of scholars to study them. For understanding the social and political reality some analytical tools are necessary. Such tools are known as the perspectives or frameworks. Any attempt to understand reality without a framework is like groping in the dark. Political scientists have used different frameworks

in order to capture and understand patterns of state politics in India. It should be noted that there are no specific frameworks meant exclusively to state politics. The same frameworks can be applied to study politics at any level of its operation---national, state or local. The categorisation of frameworks is generally known by the level at which it is applied. Thus when applied to study state politics, these frameworks can be referred to as the frameworks for the analysis of state politics. In this unit you will study about these frameworks.

SYSTEMIC FRAMEWORK   Book Q.1

Systemic framework is one of the two frameworks which have been most commonly used to analyse state politics. It is also known by its variants like structural-functional, modernisation or developmental frameworks. The other such framework is Marxian. In fact, till the 1970s these two frameworks were the predominant. As you will study in this unit, there also emerged other frameworks in the later period. But these two frameworks continue to be used in one or the other forms. Some of the later frameworks are the off-shoots of these two principal frameworks-the systemic and the Marxian. Besides, some scholars have used a combination of frameworks at the same time.

Let us begin with the systemic framework. As a part of the behavioural movement in social sciences, this framework was adopted by political scientists to study changes and order in the political systems. Developed basically in America, this framework was used to study the politics of the countries which had been liberated from the colonial rule.

The political system consists of political institutions/ structures and processes. Different constituent structures/institutions of the system keep interacting, conflicting and adjusting with each other, balancing and counter-balancing themselves. These processes occur in a social and political milieu. In such situation the political system maintains itself. It does not break down. The political system thus is resilient. Many political scientists have followed the systemic framework to study Indian politics. It has been used to study both the politics of the country as a whole and also state politics.

Caste also drew attention of political scientists like that of the sociologists. In an attempt to understand the developing or traditional societies, they strove to comprehend the interaction between the modernity and the traditions. Modernity was identified with modern political institutions and processes-elected government, nation-state, modern leadership or elite, universal adult franchise, parties, elections, etc., which were new to the newly decolonised countries.

Systemic framework has come under attack from various quarters. Its most scathing critique has been provided by the Marxist scholars. They argue that systemic framework overlooks the role of class in politics; it undermines the significance of history in political processes; it subordinates the state to the political system and does not link the politics within a country to the influence of outside forces like imperialism. They contend that systemic framework is basically anti-change and status quoist.

MARXIAN FRAMEWORKS Book Q.2

The Marxian framework analyses politics in terms of class relations or social relations of production and forces of production. It considers politics as reflection of class relations. Politics is impacted or determined by the economic relations in a society. The political institutions including the state are representatives of the class interests. And in a class divided society they serve the interests of the upper or the propertied classes. Unlike the systemic framework the Marxian framework links the politics in a developing country to the imperialism of the developed countries. The imperialism influences the politics in the developing countries by the conditionalities of the international funding agencies like the World Bank and the International Monetary Fund (IMF). As a result of these conditionalities, the states within the developing countries devise policies which adversely affect the ordinary people. Peoples' reaction to these policies form the part of class struggle against the ruling classes. There are differences among the Marxist scholars regarding the determining role of class or economic factors. In the light of these differences, the Marxian framework can be divided into two groups - classical and neo-Marxism frameworks.

➢ **Classical Marxian Framework**

The classical Marxian approach mentioned in the Communist Manifesto accords an overdetermining role to economy in relation to politics. In this case the economy is base and the politics is superstructure. Marx and Engels revised their thesis regarding the determining role of

base in The Eighteenth Bruimmiare of the Louis Bonaparte . They now believed that superstructures are not always determined by the base. The latter has its relative autonomy. But in the ultimate analysis it is the base which determines the superstructure. Thus politics has its relative autonomy.

➢ **Neo-Marxian Framework**

The Marxian perspective which gives adequate focus to the non-economic factors - culture, consciousness to the analysis of politics or any other issue is known as neo-Marxism. The neo-Marxism has emerged as a result of the influence of Gramsci, Frankfort School and Ralph Miliband. The Gramscian impact is most visible in the subaltern school. Popularised by Ranajit Guha subaltern school is significant in the study of modern Indian history. But the insights and concepts used by the subaltern school are used by individual political scientists to study the contemporary politics as well.

THE POST-MODERNIST FRAMEWORKS

Several significant political, social and economic changes have occurred in India. These changes are denoted by advancing globalisation, democratisation, decentralisation, emergence and assertion of identities based on caste, religion and ethnicity, and new social movements. These developments are being captured from various perspectives including the systemic and the Marxian. Some scholars are mixing more than one framework. But there is a growing understanding of some scholars that hitherto available frameworks are not able to explain the new features of politics. They follow the alternative frameworks, which are known as the "post- modernist" framework. Inspired by the writings of philosopher like Lyotard, postmodernism has become a significant framework of analysis for several disciplines.

Let us consider its application to the study of state politics. There is a growing understanding among some scholars that studying the political system as mega unit of analysis - nation-state, political system, party system, caste system, etc. has been impacted by the modenisation project. While in the practice politics of modernisation or modernity does not give enough autonomy to the parts of a political unit, in academic studies the impact of modernisation project or modernity is reflected in the neglect of these parts. In order to beak away from such framework of analysis, a large number of scholars emphasise the need to study the fragments of the mega units, to acknowledge their autonomy.

According to the "discourse" or "deconstructionist" perspective a narrative can be understood by breaking its contents into pieces or by deconstructing it. The best way to understand it is contexualising the narrative in terms of knowledge power and discourse formation, areas which have been theorised extensively among others by Michel Foucault. For example, in case of conflict between more than one party, it is difficult to know as to what is the truth.

FEDERATION-BUILDING FRAMEWORK

This framework is developed against the modernisation or development perspective to study the problems related to the self-determination movements - autonomy movements, insurgencies, secessionist movements and conflicts arisen because of them, in the states located in the periphery of the country, especially North-East India; it can also be applied to Jammu and Ksahmir, Punjab or any other state where self-determination movements take place.

SOCIAL CAPITAL FRAMEWORK

The rise of new social movements, civil societies and realisation to study substantive democracy has added to the significance of this perspective. In an attempt to study social capital in fragmented societies, the scholars have given significance to it. Ashutosh Varshney in his book Ethnic Conflict and Civic Life: Hindus and Muslims in India has used social capital framework to study ethnic riots in six cities of India. He argues that ethnic riots occur in the cities where the people do not have good associational relations among themselves. And they do not occur where people have associational relations. He seeks substantiate his argument with the empirical study of pairs of six cities, three of which have witnessed riots and three of which have not. In the similar vein, a large number studies which have and social capital framework to study politics in some states have been published in Interrogating Social Capital edited by Dwaipayan Bhattacharya, Niraja Jayal, Sudha Pai and Bisnu N Mahapatra. The scholars of these studies attempted to study of possibility of existence of social capital and its relationship to democracy in states of India, as a case of segmented society.

FRAMEWORKS TO STUDY ELECTIONS

Elections have been considered as the most expressive medium of existence of democracy. Indicative of only minimalist notion of democracy, elections, however, according to critics do not always prove the existence of true democracy unlike the substantive democracy. Nevertheless, elections are among the most significant features of democracy in India, at various levels of their operation - national, state or local. Their significance has got further enhanced with the increased frequency of elections in India since the last decade of the twentieth century. Elections have attracted the attention of scholars, journalists and psephologists to study electoral politics, especially at the national and state levels. The general interest in elections which mainly started in the 1960s has got further boost since the 1990s. A host of people, survey agencies, psephologists conduct surveys before and after elections to cater to the immediate need to satisfic the public curiousity as well as to provide data to analyse democracy in India.

2.2: IGNOU Book Exercise – Solved

1) Discuss how the systemic framework is used to study state politics?

Answer by India Ebook: Refer the Marked 1 Shot Concept Above.

2) Identify the basic features of the Marxian framework.

Answer by India Ebook: Refer the Marked 1 Shot Concept Above.

3) Discuss how different frameworks are applied to the study of identities, new social movements and elections in state politics.

Answer by India Ebook: The Fedaration Building framework is developed against the modernisation or development perspective to study the problems related to the self-determination movements - autonomy movements, insurgencies, secessionist movements and conflicts arisen because of them, in the states located in the periphery of the country, especially North-East India; it can also be applied to Jammu and Ksahmir, Punjab or any other state where self-determination movements take place.

The rise of **new social movements**, civil societies and realisation to study substantive democracy has added to the significance of this perspective. In an attempt to study social capital in fragmented societies, the scholars have given significance to it. Ashutosh Varshney in his book Ethnic Conflict and Civic Life: Hindus and Muslims in India has used social capital framework to study ethnic riots in six cities of India. He argues that ethnic riots occur in the cities where the people do not have good associational relations among themselves. And they do not occur where people have associational relations. He seeks substantiate his argument with the empirical study of pairs of six cities, three of which have witnessed riots and three of which have not. In the similar vein, a large number studies which have and social capital framework to study politics in some states have been published in Interrogating Social Capital edited by Dwaipayan Bhattacharya, Niraja Jayal, Sudha Pai and

Bisnu N Mahapatra. The scholars of these studies attempted to study of possibility of existence of social capital and its relationship to democracy in states of India, as a case of segmented society.

Elections have been considered as the most expressive medium of existence of democracy. Indicative of only minimalist notion of democracy, elections, however, according to critics do not always prove the existence of true democracy unlike the substantive democracy. Nevertheless, elections are among the most significant features of democracy in India, at various levels of their operation - national, state or local. Their significance has got further enhanced with the increased frequency of elections in India since the last decade of the twentieth century. Elections have attracted the attention of scholars, journalists and psephologists to study electoral politics, especially at the national and state levels. The general interest in elections which mainly started in the 1960s has got further boost since the 1990s. A host of people, survey agencies, psephologists conduct surveys before and after elections to cater to the immediate need to satisfic the public curiousity as well as to provide data to analyse democracy in India.

2.3: IGNOU Past 6 Attempts Question – Solved

Dec 2020: Briefly describe the systemic and post-modernist frameworks to analyse State politics in India.2 Q.1 +

Answer by India Ebook: Almost Same as Q.1 plus Post-Modenist.

June 2021: Discuss the Marxian approach to study state politics. 2 Q.2

Answer by India Ebook: Exact Same as Q.2 of Above.

3. NATURE OF INDIAN DIVERSITIES AND NATIONALIST RESPONSES

Introduction
Caste, Untouchability and Oppressive Diversity
Religious Diversity Versus Communalism
Language: Homogeneity or Plurality?
Tribal Revolt: Civilise and Preserve?

3.1: One Shot Concepts

INTRODUCTION

Nehru's catch-phrase 'unity-in-diversity' is perhaps best reflective of modern nationalist responses to the challenges posed by diversities. Travelling through India on the eve of the general elections of 1937, Nehru discovered and enthused about the natural and cultural diversity that he found everywhere - in the physical layout of the land as well as the physical appearances of the people, in their cultural habits and religious differences. But underlying this diversity, he had 'glimpses' of a 'dream of unity'. This unity was not visible in external standardisation of beliefs or customs but was 'something deeper'. It was not just an intellectual unity but an emotional unity to be experienced.

Did this unity really exist 'out there' in the world?

It is important to note that Nehru wrote of the 'dream' of unity; like any dream, it called for active imagination and effort on our part. Like him, most nationalists saw mind-boggling diversities and dreamt of a unity; but like all dreams, their dream was continuously interrupted, distorted and shaped by the realities of politics.

CASTE, UNTOUCHABILITY AND OPPRESSIVE DIVERSITY

Book Q.1

Caste identity, either as a fourfold order or as jati could not simply be celebrated as an expression of Indian diversity. But it did not become the subject of an explicit national campaign until the early years of the twentieth century. Bhikhu Parekh has noted that as Indian nationalists began to demand social and political equality from colonial government, the fact that such equality was denied to many within the Hindu society had also to be faced. A second political reason was that Hindu leaders began to see that internal divisions and disunity had to be overcome in order to wage an effective struggle against colonialism. Lala Lajpat Rai lamented how untouchability had caused many to convert thereby increasing the numerical strength of the Muslims and Christians. He warned that Hindus might become minorities in their own country unless they set their house in order. Thus untouchability slowly but definitely became a matter of shame, a 'blot' on Hindu conscience to be removed. Despite widespread consensus on the issue, the Congress did not pass a resolution condemning untouchability.

B. R. Ambedkar launched the most devastating critique of this position claiming that caste was an integral part of Hinduism, that there was nothing rational or ethical or efficient about classifying people as superior or inferior at birth, that untouchability was an integral part of the caste system and that none of these could be simply reformed away without a major overhaul of the religion itself. He reminded that even enlightened saints and seers like Samkara or Ramanuja never attacked social inequality, only inequality before God. Ambedkar's wrestling with this question and his final exit from Hinduism are telling in this regard.

RELIGIOUS DIVERSITY VERSUS COMMUNALISM

Book Q.2 & 3

The Indian nationalists had to contend with diversity and differences within religions as well as between religions within the Indian context. Most nationalists, whether they were Hindu revivalists like Tilak or liberals like Nehru explicitly rejected the idea of a majoritarian rule based on one religion or language. On the surface, they eschewed thinking of the nation in terms of a single religious identity.

At a general level, religious diversity, in itself, was not a problem; in fact, it was cherished as a unique manifestation of Indian, more specifically Hindu, toleration. But communalism, that is, a 'narrow group mentality basing itself on a religious community but in reality concerned with political power and patronage of the interested group' was a problem fuelled by the divide and rule policy of the British.

But then few nationalists managed to transcend communal thinking and preserve diversity within and between religions. Hindu revivalists such as Tilak considered diversity within Hinduism as inhibiting Hindu unity to some extent. Sectarian prejudices were seen as weakening the Hindu community. Further, Tilak's vision of the future where he saw the Hindus united into a strong community also had to be examined.

In contrast, Gandhi forged a nationalist response that was relatively more inclusive and less aggressive vis-à-vis other religions. Besides the Gita, he appealed to other sources such as Sermon on the Mount, Jain ideal of ahimsa and Vaishnavist bhakti. Gandhi continued to conceive of the Indian nation based on Hindu ideals such as swaraj or Ram Rajya. But through the ideal of non-violent action, he hoped to temper the assertive impulse from turning into aggressive Hindu nationalism. His vision of Hindu community did not require new temples on disputed sites.

A third ideological response to religious diversity came from liberal secular persons such as Nehru. For Nehru, Muslims were not a community opposed to the Hindu community. He saw them as equally divided by class, language and ideologies. Similarly, he did not see the Hindus as a homogeneous community. As noted above, he was more concerned about this kind of thinking leading to conflict.

The reform movements among Hindus and Muslims helped them acquire a sense of communal identity. Hindu communalism was made possible thanks to reform movements. In the early part this century, Dayanand Saraswati's Arya Samaj succeeded in combining the earlier social reform issues (opposition to child marriage, idolatry, polytheism, widowhood taboos, brahminical dominance etc.) with a pan-Hindu consciousness. Along with shuddhi campaigns, they gained deep roots among a variety of caste groups. By the 1890s the Arya Samaj was beginning to criticise the Congress for not being Hindu enough and held conferences at Kumbh Melas and Sanatan Dharma Sabhas. Elsewhere, Ramakrishna Mission in Bengal, Prarthana Samaj in Pune region and Theosophical society in Madras also promoted a sense of Hindu community through their revivalist practices.

LANGUAGE:HOMOGENEITY OR PLURALITY?

At an ideological level, it appeared obvious to many that there had to be a 'national' or 'official' language' though there was no need for a national or official religion. What about continuing English as the official language? Even Nehru claimed that it was a foreign language and was not known to large masses of our people. But he took a moderate position on the replacement of English.

In general, many nationalists like Tilak found the diversity of languages an obstacle to national unity and urged the need for a common language.

He suggested that the Devanagari script may be used for all northern languages. Subsequently, the north-centred composition of the Congress and the influence of Hindu Mahasabha contributed to Hindi in the Nagari script being elevated into a possible national language for Free India.

Gandhi too was keen on promoting Hindi especially in the South. But the southern experience was ahead in this regard. In 1938, Rajagopalachari, the then premier of Madras had introduced Hindi whether in Nagari or Urdu script as an optional subject or as he put it 'chutney on a leaf—take it or leave it'.

Hindi-supporters were to insist upon adoption of Hindi as official language. The 'Hindi extremists' produced a Hindi constitution which even Hindi speakers from North India found hard to understand given the sanskritisation of the same. Finally consensus emerged over the continued use of English for at least fifteen years until the1960's agitations over the issue again.

A second issue to emerge was that of linguistic provinces. Given that the British created multilingual states to forestall unity, the Congress had agreed in principle to creation of linguistic states. But Nehru was to move slowly on this issue after independence and it only assumed salience in the 1950s.

TRIBAL REVOLTS : CIVILISE AND PRESERVE?

Tribal communities have always revolted often and violently in India. Instead of being primitive savages confined to the forest, tribals are integrated into Indian society as the lowest stratum as agricultural labourers, coolies and so on. Commercialisation of forests, land grabbing and increasing immiseration saw many revolts such as Santal rebellion (1855), Munda rebellion (1895-1900) and the Alluri Sitarama Raju movement in Godavari region in 1922-24 to mention a few.

The nationalists approached tribals primarily as illiterate masses to be 'civilized' and enlisted into the mainstream. As with other lower caste groups, nationalists did not think of them as autonomous agents creating their own history or as groups which might have had agendas different from the Congress. This meant that at a practical level they were mobilised and demobilised as per the needs of the Congress. This was evident in the case of Midnapur adivasi rebellion between 1921-1923.

The Congress began enlisting advasis in this region only around 1921 and successfully organised a strike against very low wages.

The Congress undoubtedly channelised existing discontent among the adivasis and extended it against paddy exports and foreign cloth. But subsequently the struggle assumed its own dynamism during Non-cooperation and the adivasis took to looting select stores. The withdrawal of Noncooperation meant that their struggle was denied external links; so when the adivasis rebelled again in 1922 for traditional jungle rights, they were acting autonomously and Congress only backed them indirectly.

This paternalism flowed into the Constitutional settlement where there were several protectionist measures so as to preserve and protect the interests of the Scheduled Tribes. Article 15 which bans discrimination on grounds of race, caste, etc., explicitly allows for some provisions to advance SCs and STs. Artilce 19(5) dealing with freedom of residence allows special restrictions to promote the interests of STs in some restricted areas. Similarly there are provisions for a special officer, national commission and special grants-in-aid.

3.2: IGNOU Book Exercise - Solved

1) Discuss the ways in which nationalists responded to caste and untouchability. Were these responses shaped by the upper-caste biases of the nationalists as Ambedkar or Periyar would claim?

Answer by India Ebook: Refer the Marked 1 Shot Concept Above.

2) How did the nationalists respond to religious diversity and communalism?

Answer by India Ebook: Refer the Marked 1 Shot Concept Above.

3) Critically analyse the main arguments of this unit regarding the adequacy of nationalist responses to different kinds of diversity?

Answer by India Ebook: Refer the Marked 1 Shot Concept Above.

3.3: IGNOU Past 6 Attempts Question - Solved

HHHH

B B B B B

4. STATES IN THE CONSTITUTIONAL SCHEME

4.1: One Shot Concepts

INTRODUCTION

The framers of the Indian Constitution created a federal state, structured essentially on the model of the Government of India Act, 1935, in recognition of the enormous diversity of the regions of this vast sub-continent. It was a highly centralised federation. However, political forces have worked towards reducing the Centre's grip over the states. And there is increasing realisation of the need for coordination between the two sets of government.

BACKGROUND

When we speak of 'States in the Constitutional Scheme' we mean by the 'state' a unit of the Indian state that is structured on the federal pattern as in the United States of America (USA). The federating states of the USA were independent states before the formation of the US

federation in 1789. After the formation of the USA its units continued to be called 'states'. All the federations that were formed after 1789 did not call their units states. The units of the Swiss confederation are called 'cantons,' a French word meaning provinces. The Canadian federation calls its units 'provinces' whereas in the former Union of Soviet Socialist Republics they were called republics.

Before India became free and framed her republican constitution it was the territories under the rule of the native princes which were called 'princely states.' The territories within British India were divided into provinces. The Constitution of India removed this difference of status and organised India into four kinds of states A, B, C and D. After 1956 the units of the Indian federation came to be classified under two broad categories, alled 'states' and 'Union territories.' Subsequently, several Union territories were promoted to the status of states. Union territories may, therefore, be regarded as potential states. An understanding of the state system in India is focused broadly on three themes:

1) Identity and territorial integrity of the states.

2) Relation of the states with the Union of India.

3) Relation among the states.

IDENTITY AND TERRITORIAL INTEGRITY OF STATES

Identity and territorial integrity of the states is of course the basic feature of the state system. Technically it would mean that the states which form the federation should retain their shape, name and character. In practice, however, this is always not so. Even in the world's classic federation, the USA, the identity and territorial shape of the states have changed a great deal over time – specifically between the formation of the federation (1789) and the civil war of the 1860s.

In India the years since Independence have seen many a great change in the shape, identity and character of the states. The main reason for this is that the British left India as a highly amorphous country. Its economy was fragmented and variegated. Its administrative units did not correspond to the cultural contours of the Indian population. Its administrative pattern was not uniform. The political leadership of independent India had to sort out these divergences which still persist. The reorganisation of states is yet incomplete.

Constitution of new states, their mergers and the changes of their territorial boundaries have been facilitated by **Article 3** of the Constitution which allows the Parliament to:

(a) form new states by separation of territory from any state or by uniting two or more states or parts of states or by uniting any territory to a part of any state;

(b) increase the area of any state;

(c) diminish the area of any state;

(d) alter the boundaries of any state; an (a) alter the name of any state; after the President (i.e., the Union Government) has so recommended after consultation with the state legislature(s) concerned.

One aspect of the states' identity is that, unlike in the USA, in India, there is no double citizenship. There is only the citizenship of the Union.

UNION-STATE RELATIONSHIP

The Indian Constitution elaborately lays down this division of power in the Seventh Schedule under **Article 246**. Broadly speaking, the matters necessary to run a unified administration and areas of common interest of the states are placed in the **Union List** (*List I*) and the matters of particular interests of the states are placed in the **State List** (*List II*). There is a third list of subjects under a **Concurrent List** (*List III*) on which the Union and the states have concurrent jurisdiction.

The Concurrent List, it should be understood, does not mean that these powers are exercised by the Union and the states in cooperation with each other. There are other provisions in the Constitution of India enabling such cooperation. Nor does the Concurrent List mean that the Union and the states can exercise their authority on matters included in it subject to concurrence (i.e., consent) of each other. Concurrent subjects are those subjects on which both the Union and the states exercise their jurisdiction.

Generally speaking, the Union has **power over all matters** of defence, including the armed forces and their deployment; atomic energy and the minerals; war and peace; foreign affairs and foreign jurisdiction; admission into, expulsion and emigration from India; pilgrimage abroad; railways; national highways; national waterways; maritime shipping and navigation; major ports; airways; post, telegraph and telephone; currency, coinage and foreign exchange and many more.

Generally speaking, the **states have jurisdiction** over public order and police without involving the Union's armed forces; officers and servants of the High Courts; prisons; local government; public health and sanitation; pilgrimage inside India; intoxicating liquors; relief of disabled and unemployable; burial and burial grounds; cremations and cremation grounds; libraries, museums, ancient and historical monuments other than those of national importance, roads, bridges, ferries and other means of communication outside the scope of the Union list.

➢ The Extra-ordinary Powers of Parliament

Governmental activities are conducted in terms of law. The primary focus of the division of power between the Union and states, therefore, falls on legislation. Executive powers of the Union and the states are co-extensive with their legislative powers. There is no doubt about the fact that the division of power between the Union and the states is heavily loaded in favour of the Union. This load has been increased by certain extraordinary provisions of the Constitution.

According to **Article 249** of the Constitution the parliament may legislate on any subject, if the Council of States (Rajya Sabha), by a two –thirds majority declares such subject to be a subject of national importance. According to **Article 250** the parliament may legislate on any state subject, for the whole or any part of the territory of India, during the operation of a proclamation of emergency.

According to **Article 252** the parliament may legislate on a state subject for two or more states if their legislatures consider it desirable. On the other hand, as the Union may legislate on its jurisdictional subjects for the whole or a part of the country, there is no provision for the Union delegating its power to legislate to any state legislature(s).

In case of a declaration of constitutional breakdown in a state under **Article 356** of the Constitution, not only the legislative functions of the state legislature but also its financial powers are taken over by the parliament. That is to say, the parliament passes its budgets, allocates fund for administration and controls taxation for the state government.

➢ The Extra-ordinary Executive Powers of the Union Book Q.2

The executive powers of the Union and the states are coextensive with their respective legislative powers which, we have seen are heavily tilted towards the Union. The extra-ordinary excutive powers of the Union are, however, more than this range of powers by way of certain special provisions of the Constitution.

The executive power of the states are required to be so exercised as not to impede or prejudice the executive power of the Union. The most important of such powers is the appointment and removal of the governors of the states who may, as we shall see, become their real executive heads on occasions. The Union can give executive directions to the states toward that purpose.

The executive power of the Union will also extend to the giving of directions to a state as to the construction and maintenance of means of communication declared in the direction to be of national or military importance and of the protection of the railways **Article 257** according to **Article 365** the failure of a state to comply with and give effect to such directions may entitle it to the declaration of constitutional breakdown by the Union.

➢ **The Governor's Role** Book Q.3

The state Governor has a critical role in maintaining the status and autonomy of the states. The Governor is appointed by the President of India (i.e., the Union) and holds his/her tenure during the pleasure of the President. He is the agent of the Union and is normally expected to secure the Union-state amity. At times, however, his role may turn out to be a major factor of tension in the Union-state relation.

The Governor is the executive head of the state and all functions of the state executive are carried out in his name and under his authority. He appoints a Council of Ministers to aid and advise him on his functions except when he is required under the constitution to act in his discretion. This exception is not there in the case of the President of India in whose case all ministerial advises are binding.

On the other hand, the Council of Ministers is responsible to the elected state legislature. It has reason to claim to be representatives of the people of the state. Whenever the governor overrides the state council of Ministers, therefore, a suppression of democracy is alleged.

The problem becomes complicated by two special powers of the Governor:

(1) the power to reserve bills, after they are passed by the state legislature, for the President's assent, and

(2) the power to report a breakdown of the constitutional machinery.

There is no clear answer to that Should the Governor exercise these powers on the aid and advice of the Council of Ministers However, it can be assumed that a Governor can never expect his/her council of Ministers to report a constitutional breakdown in the state, and he/she must do it without the Council of Minister's advice. This cannot be said about the first power. If a state legislation is expected to be controversial, a governor may try to persuade the council of Ministers to advise him/her to reserve the bill for the President's assent. Exercise of these two powers by the Governor has created great bitterness in Union-state relations.

➢ The Administrative Relations

Government is largely run by the bureaucracy. There are three kinds of bureaucracy in India: the state services, the central services and the all-India services. Whereas the first two services are filled up and controlled by the states and centre respectively, the all-India services are filled up and largely controlled by the centre though the officers are attached to the state cadre. Senior positions in the state governments are almost always manned by members of the all-India services, namely, the Indian Administrative Service and the Indian Police Service. However, members of the all-India services as well as the central services are recruited through the Union Public Service Commission while the members of the state services are recruited through the State Public Service Commission in each state.

There are two special kinds of bureaucrats whose status is constitutional: the Comptroller and Auditor-General of India and the Election Commissioners of India. They are appointed by the President of India. The Comptroller and Auditor-General examines the accounts of both the Union and the state Governments. The Election Commission supervises the elections at the central and the state levels. This allows some control of the Union over the government accounts and the election processes in the states.

➢ The Financial Status of the States

Generally speaking, all taxes and duties collected by the states go to their coffer and are appropriated by the states. They include such stamp duties and such duties of excise on medicinal and toilet preparations as are mentioned in the Union list that are levied by the Union but collected and appropriated by the states where they are levied (Article 268).

The revenues and taxes collected by the Union, from the items mentioned in the Union list, however, are appropriated in two ways. The taxes on sale and purchase of goods and taxes on consignment of goods other than newspapers of inter-state nature are levied and collected by the Union but assigned to the states where they are collected and distributed among those states according to the principles laid down by Parliament (Article 269).

All other taxes and duties under the Union list are levied and collected by the Union and distributed between the Union and the states
according to the manner prescribed by the Finance Commission or, until the Finance Commission is constituted, by the President (Article 270).

There are two items mentioned in the Concurrent list, namely, (1) Stamp duties other than duties or fees collected by means of judicial stamps, but not including rates of stamp duties, and (2) fees in respect of any matters in respect of the matters in the concurrent list, but not including fees taken in any court, which belong to concurrent jurisdiction of the Union and the states. Their proceeds are retained by the Union and the states respectively. The Union may collect any duty or tax from matters not mentioned in any of the lists and retain their proceeds.

For a long time the Finance Commission used to make recommendation only on non-plan expenditure of the governments. Since the ninth Finance Commission they are making recommendations on plan expenditures too.

> ➤ **Tension Areas in Union-State Relations**   Book Q.5

It has been noticed that the Union-state conflicts relate mainly to division of financial resources between them, the role of the Governor, particularly in giving assent to legislations by the state legislatures, appointment and dismissal of the Council of Ministers and recommendations of President's rule on the ground of 'constitutional breakdown.' Most of these are political questions and, for long, the Supreme court declined to intervene in such disputes. In 1993, however, in the case of S.R. Bommai and Others vs. the Union of India, the Supreme Court decided that the relevance of material contained in the report of the Governor recommending the President's rule in a state is subject to judicial scrutiny. In any case, the state legislature cannot be dissolved until after the Parliament debates and approves of the declaration of constitutional breakdown. In 1998, in the case of Uttar Pradesh the Supreme Court ordered a floor test of the strength of the parties claiming the right to be appointed to the Government.

For a long time the states have complained about their meagre financial resources that made them rely heavily upon the grants-in-aid by the Union as well as loans sanctioned by it. The 80th amendment to the Constitution effected in the year 2000 sought to remove part of the imbalance by making more fund available from the Union coffers to the states. But the principles by which the Finance Commission divide the state allocations have not satisfied the states. The rich states complain that they are deprived of their legitimate share of the Central transfers, the poor states complain that they are not getting enough.

INTER-STATE RELATIONS Book Q.6

The Constitution envisaged a relation of peaceful coexistence, if not amicable co-operative relations among the member states of the federation. If there arises any dispute between the Union and a state or a group of states or the Union and a state or a group of states on the one side and one or more states on the other; or between two or more states, the Supreme Court of India can be approached under its original jurisdiction for adjudication (**Article 131**). There are two specific mechanisms prescribed for resolution of inter-state disputes outside the judicial process however:

1) Parliament may by law provide for the adjudication of any dispute or complaint with respect to the use, distribution or control of the waters or, or in, any inter-state river or river valley (**Article 262**).

2) If at any time it appears to the President that public interest would be served by the establishment of a Council charges with the duty of – (a) inquiring into and advising upon disputes which may have arisen between states; (investigating and discussing subjects in which all or some states , or the Union and one or more states, have a common interest; or (c) making recommendations upon any subject and, in particular, recommendations for the better coordination of policy and action with respect to that subject – it shall be lawful for the President by

order to establish such a Council, and to define the nature of the duties to be performed by it and its organisation and procedure (**Article 263**).

The Inter-State Council has discussed the desirability of controlling the power of the Union to declare a constitutional breakdown in a state under **Article 356** of the Constitution and has recommended the restriction of this power through amendment of the Constitution.

Parliament has the power to set up tribunals to decide inter-state river disputes and it can, by legislation, exclude the jurisdiction of any court in the matter. Such tribunals in the past have not been entirely successful as they do not have the judicial authority to enforce their decision. On the other hand, under the **River Waters Disputes Act, 1956**, the Supreme Court can direct the Central Government to fulfil its statutory obligation.

The most difficult point of inter-state conflict is the border disputes between the states arising out of historical and cultural factors. Occasionally such conflicts have led to violence as in the dispute between Karnataka and Maharashtra. The constitutional mechanism to solve the dispute is provided by **Article 3** of the Constitution which vests the power of altering the boundaries of states only after receiving the views of the concerned states. Parliament is not obliged to respect the views, but to disregard them may be politically disastrous.

POLITICS AND STATE RIGHTS

Much of the autonomy of the states, their rights against the Centre as well as against each other depends upon politics. The Central Government can persuade the state Governments to accept a certain point of view if both the Governments are under the control of the same party. The massive states reorganisation of 1956, the partition of Gujarat and Maharashtra in 1960, the partition of Punjab in 1966 and the reorganisation of north-east India in 1971 were possible because the Congress party was in power at the Centre and at the concerned states at the relevant times.

When different parties are at the Centre and at the states, ideological and political conflicts often create tension between the Centre and the states as well as among the states. Since 1959 a number of state governments have been superseded chiefly because they were run by parties other than the one that ruled the Centre. The grossest cases occurred in 1977, when the Janata Party government at the Centre dissolved as many as eight state governments government run by the Congress Party. In 1980, on the other hand, the Congress-run central government superseded as many state governments run by the Janata Party. After that, however, the frequency of such supersessions decreased and, in 1993, the practice got severely restricted by the Bommai case judgement of the Supreme court of India.

In 1989 one-party hegemony (of the Congress Party) was decisively over. Except for the period of 1991-96 the Central Government came to be controlled by coalitions in which regional parties played major roles. Consequently, central intervention in state affairs also fell substantially. Two major complaints of the states, however, persist: (1) the Centre is accused of putting party men at the gubernatorial positions in the states to serve its own political agenda, and (2) the Centre discriminates against some states and favours some in regard to financial support on party considerations.

4.2: IGNOU Book Exercise - Solved

1) To what extent did the Constitution envisage the autonomy of the states in the Indian federal structure in regard to the legislative division of power?

Answer by India Ebook: Refer the Marked 1 Shot Concept Above.

2) What is the extent of executive control of the Union over the states in India?

Answer by India Ebook: Refer the Marked 1 Shot Concept Above.

3) Examine the **role of the Governor** in Union-State Relation.

Answer by India Ebook: Refer the Marked 1 Shot Concept Above.

4) Examine the financial status of the states in the Indian federation.

Answer by India Ebook: Refer the Marked 1 Shot Concept Above.

5) Examine the **tension areas** in the Union-State relations.

Answer by India Ebook: Refer the Marked 1 Shot Concept Above.

6) What kinds of inter-state conflicts are envisaged in the Constitution of India? What are the mechanisms prescribed for solution of such conflicts?

Answer by India Ebook: Refer the Marked 1 Shot Concept Above.

4.3: IGNOU Past 6 Attempts Question - Solved

June 2019: Discuss Centre-State relations in Contemporary Indian Politics. Answer by India Ebook: Almost same as Q.5 above.

5. DEVELOPMENT OF STATE SYSTEM

Introduction

Dynamics of Indian Federalism

- ➤ Annexation and Territorial Arrangement of British India
- ➤ Amorphousness of the British Empire
- ➤ Centralisation of Government

The Post-Colonial Experience

- ➤ Constitutional Arrangement in Independent India
- ➤ Origin of Linguism in India
- ➤ Language and State Boundaries
- ➤ Ethnic States
- ➤ Reasons for Statehood Demand

Statehood and Power

- ➤ The Horizontal Problems of Statehood
- ➤ The Union-State Relations
- ➤ Constitutional Amendments

5.1: One Shot Concepts

INTRODUCTION

The State System in independent India emerged within a broadly federal framework. It is true that the term 'federal' does not occur in the Constitution of India. In fact, very few federal constitutions of the world use this term specifically. The Unites States of America is acknowledged to be the oldest and a classical federal constitution. It does not use the term federal or federation.

The **USA** is a 'union of states.' So is India (according to Article 1 of the Indian Constitution). Both countries are organised in a federal structure. That means, essentially, that in both the countries, as well as in all federations, there are two levels of government, that power is divided between the two by a written constitution and that there is an independent judiciary to supervise that division of power.

DYNAMICS OF INDIAN FEDERALISM   June 2021

Text books on the Indian Constitution usually try to establish a historical linkage between the Indian Constitution and the Government of India Act, 1935. It will, however, be wrong to see the Indian federal set-up of today as a replica of the 1935 Act. The Government of India Act, 1935, was based on the principle of devolution of power from the British sovereign through the Governor-General. Provincial autonomy that was sanctioned by that Act was severely circumscribed.

The present Indian Constitution vests the sovereignty decisively in the people of India. In fact, the premier Indian political party, the Indian National Congress worked under that Act for only about three years, and that too only at the provincial level.

The other significant feature of the Indian federation of today is that the shape of its component units has been changing. This, however, is not unique to the Indian Constitution. Although, in 1863, President Abraham Lincoln declared that the United States is 'an indestructible union of indestructible states,' the shape of the states of that country was continuously changing up to the civil war of the 1860s. That process is continuing in India.

The main reason why the shape of the states of the USA- went on changing for nearly a century was the annexation of territories from the native people of America during this period. In India a somewhat similar process caused the change in the territorial shape of the country as well as its units of government. Broadly speaking this process was the result of the British colonial rule.

> ➢ **Annexations and Territorial Arrangement of British India**

Book Q.1

Until 1765 British presence in India was mainly through leases and Zamindaris. In 1661 the British had got hold of Bombay as a dowry from the Portuguese royalty to the English king Charles II. In 1765 the East India Company got the dewani of the Bengal suba from emperor Shah Alam. After the fall of Tipu Sultan Madras and the neighbouring territories were annexed.

After the third Anglo-Maratha war of 1803 they came to control the districts of Agra and the territory of Delhi. In 1836 the Nawab of Oudh was made to cede the Benares area which was joined with the conquered districts and the territory of Delhi and Agra to form the North Western Provinces. Oudh itself was annexed in 1856 and joined with Bengal. It was constituted as a Chief Commissioner's Province in 1856. In 1858 Delhi was transferred to Punjab. In 1877 Oudh was merged with the North Western Provinces. In 1912 Delhi was separated from Punjab as the imperial capital and a Chief Commissioner's Province.

In 1826, after the first Anglo-Burmese war, Assam was annexed. Sind was conquered in 1842 and the Punjab territories in 1859. Meanwhile, in 1853, Berar was annexed from Hyderabad, but, in return of the services of the Nizam in 1857, was returned to him.

In 1861 the Central Provinces was constituted by uniting the lapsed Bhonsle (Maratha) kingdom of Nagpur and territories transferred from the North Western District. In 1903 the Nizam was made to cede Berar again and it was joined with the Chief Commissioner's Province of the

Central Provinces that had been formed in 1861 with territories mostly annexed from the Marhatta rulers. The last annexation was of Oudh in 1856. In 1858 Queen Victoria promised not to annex any more territories of the Indian Princes.

➢ Amorphousness of the British Empire

Having conquered Ceylon (today's Sri Lanka) from the Dutch the British administered it as a part of the Madras presidency till 1803. They ruled Burma as part of British India till 31 March 1937 after which it became a separate Crown Colony. Even the distant Arab port town of Aden was made a part of the Bombay Presidency after its annexation in 1839 and a Chief Commissioner's Province in British India in 1932, to be separated as a Crown Colony in 1935.

In 1947 the British partitioned British India into India and Pakistan leaving the rest of India into 566 princely states and two 'tribal areas' beyond the north western and the north eastern frontiers of British India free to join either of the countries. 554 princely states and one tribal area in the north east became parts of independent India. Subsequently the small French and Portuguese colonial possessions in the sub-continent joined India. In 1974 Sikkim, an Indian dependency since the British days, joined India.

The external boundaries of British India were never clearly demarcated. In 1902 the British enforced the Durand Line with Afghanistan splitting the tribal region lying between them. Afghanistan never acknowledged the legitimacy of the border. In 1914 they drew the Macmahon Line on the north eastern borders with Tibet, which China never acknowledged, while the western part of the northern border was left undefined. (After Independence Pakistan has been having problem with Afghanistan on the Durand Line and India has problem with China with the Macmahon Line). Some of these border territories were never administered by the British.

➢ Centralisation of Government

The early administration of British possessions in India was organised in the form of Presidencies – properties of the President of the Board of Control of the English East India Company - Bengal, Bombay and Madras. Though Madras was the oldest of these Presidencies, Bengal was the biggest – encompassing united Bengal (i.e., including today's Bangla Desh), Bihar and Orissa. The governing authority on these Presidencies was vested in three Governors. The Regulating Act of 1773 declared the Governor of Bengal as the Governor-General of British India. By the Charter Act of 1833 civil and military authority of the Governors of Bombay and Madras was transferred to the Governor-General. Legislative powers were returned to the Governors of Bombay and Madras by the Indian Councils Act of 1861. However, separate military commands in Bombay and Madras were abolished only in 1893. Meanwhile, in 1853, a Lieutenant-Governor was appointed for Bengal separating the direct administration of Bengal from the Governor-General.

At the turn of the 19th century Lord Curzon concentrated much power in the hands of the Governor-General. However, in 1909, the Morley-Minto Reforms ushered in a decentralising trend which was confirmed by the report of the Decentralisation Commission in 1912. The Montagu-Chelmsford Report carried on the decentralisation further and introduced an amount of responsible government in the form of diarchy at the provinces. Provincial autonomy was formally established by the Government of India Act, 1935. But it had several shortcomings.

THE POST-COLONIAL EXPERIENCE

> **Constitutional Arrangement in Independent India** Book Q.3

It fell upon the **Constituent Assembly** of India to organise this loose administrative-political structure within a rational framework. The immediate task was integration of the princely states. The Constituent Assembly created four kinds of States – in place of Provinces and Princely states. The major provinces of the British days that were left in India either in full (Bihar, Bombay, the Central Provinces and Berar, Madras, Orissa and the United Provinces, renamed as Uttar Pradesh) or in parts (Assam, East Punjab and West Bengal) were renamed as **Part A States**, some of the former princely states being merged with Punjab. The major princely states that joined India were constituted as **Part B States**. The smaller princely states that joined India were merged and constituted as **Part C** States along with some of the old Chief Commissioner's Provinces.

The extremely backward Andaman and Nicobar Islands were constituted as a **Part D State**. The executive heads of the Part A States were designated as Governors. The executive heads of the Part B states were designated as Raj Pramukhs. They would be ruled like the Part A States with legislatures and Councils of Ministers. The executive head of a Part C State would be either a Chief Commissioner or a Lieutenant-Governor. Parliament could create legislatures and Councils of Advisers/Ministers in such states. The Part D State of Andaman and Nicobar would be governed by the President of India through a Chief Commissioner.

Special administrative arrangements were made for the backward tracts under Schedules V and VI of the Constitution. The hitherto un-administered Naga Tribal Area and the North Eastern Frontier Tracts were placed in the Sixth Schedule, as Part B Tribal Areas, to be directly administered by the Central Government through the Governor of Assam as his agent. The Part A Tribal Areas got Autonomous District Councils while the Scheduled Areas under the Fifth Schedule were granted special provision for protection of tribal interests. While the Sixth Schedule was confined to Assam, the fifth Schedule was spread over mainly the central Indian states.

> ### Origins of Linguism in India

In 1904 Lord Curzon decided that the size of the province of Bengal was too unwieldy. He, therefore, decided to partition it. The criterion for partition would be the religious division of the Indian population. In 1905 he created a Muslim-majority province of Eastern Bengal and Assam and a non-Muslim majority province of Western Bengal. It split the Bengali-speaking population down the middle and produced a strong anti-partition movement – that actually lifted the Indian national movement to a new height. The partition was annulled in 1912 but a composite province of Bihar and Orissa was carved out of the former Bengal. The imperial capital was shifted from Calcutta to Delhi.

In 1936 Bihar and Orissa were separated as two different provinces and a new province of Sind was carved out of the province of Bombay largely on consideration of the religiouscommunal composition of the region and partly because of its lack of contiguity with the province of Bombay. In 1937 the North-West Frontier Province was granted a legislature.

Meanwhile, the anti-partition agitation in Bengal inspired linguistic aspirations on other parts of India like the Andhra region of the Madras province and Orissa. The 1920 Congress Constitution organised the party units on the basis of language and, in 1930, the Madras session of the Congress adopted the demand for linguistic provinces. While acquiescing in the creation of Sind the All-Party Conference (1928) acknowledged that Sindhi was a distinct language.

> ### Language and State Boundaries

The trauma of Partition of British India, however, made the Constituent Assembly hesitate to grant linguistic states immediately and the post-partition boundaries of the former British provinces were retained. In 1953 the Andhra agitation burst out resulting in the fast by death of a Gandhian leader, Potti Sriramalu. The state of Andhra was created in the same year. This was followed by the appointment of a States Reorganisation Commission (SRC) in 1955. The SRC recommended conversion of the four kinds of states into two categories States and Union territories and merger of the erstwhile Part B state of Hyderabad with Andhra. These two recommendations were accepted. Territorial adjustments were made to the benefit of Kerala (earlier called Travancore-Cochin), Madhya Pradesh and Mysore. Kerala and Mysore were promoted to the status of states as were Rajasthan (a conglomerate of former princely states created in 1952) and Jammu and Kashmir. Other border adjustments were made between neighbouring states too.

The demand for linguistic states was not satisfied in 1956. Agitations in Bombay led to its partitioning between Maharashtra and Gujarat in 1960 and of Punjab into Panjab and Haryana in 1966, while a part of its territory was joined with Himachal Pradesh. Territorial adjustments continued and are not yet over.

➢ The Ethnic States

1963 saw the emergence of what may be called 'ethnic states' with the creation of Nagaland. The Nagas speak about 25 languages. In 1970 an 'autonomous state' of Meghalaya was created with the autonomous tribal districts of United Khas-Jaintia Hills and Garo Hills. In 1972,

through the North Eastern Areas Reorganisation Act, 1971, Meghalaya was promoted to the status of a full state with some non-tribal areas joined with it. The former Union territories of Manipur and Tripura were promoted to the status of full states too while two Union territories were carved out of Assam to form new Union territories:

(1) the former centrally-administered North-East Frontier Tracts, with the name of Arunachal Pradesh and

(2) the Mizo Hills District with the name of Mizoram.

In 1986 Mizoram and Arunachal Pradesh became full states. In 1987 Goa earned this status.

In the year 2001 three new states were created: Chhattisgarh, carved out of Madhya Pradesh, Jharkhand carved out of Bihar and Uttaranchal carved out of Uttar Pradesh. While the first two have a tribal base, the current majority of the population is predominantly non-tribal. Uttaranchal has virtually no tribal presence. These states may appropriately be called hill states. Regional, ethnic and linguistic demands for statehood still persist in different parts of India.

➢ Reasons for Statehood Demand   Book Q.4

Closely related to the British departure is the explosion of democracy in India. By one stroke universal adult franchise was introduced in India with two exceptions of the Andaman and Nicobar Islands and the North-East Frontier Tracts of Assam. The process of democratisation through the Constitution was boosted by the process of land reform which greatly weakened, if not totally eliminated, the traditionally dominant big landlords and brought economic power to the middle and small landowners.

In the post-independence period too development planning remained uneven at least until the Fourth Five-Year Plan. Meanwhile, the green revolution in agriculture started in selected places like north western

India. The areas neglected by early planning, like north-east India, became the centres of poverty and protest.

Even the developed regions had their own complaints. Thus Punjab bore two grudges with the economic scenario. It protested against levy on crops, charges on electricity and water supplied from the major irrigation projects and the absence of the freedom to trade with foreign countries in their agricultural products. It also complained about the lack of industrialisation of the region due to the non-availability of investment in industry of the region. A more or less similar demand is now working behind the movement for a Harit Pradesh in western Uttar Pradesh.

Developmental work, following intensification of administration, spread education and political consciousness, brought about a new social revolution. A new group of literati came to lead the respective communities. Self-government for them would mean more jobs, even as politicians, more power for the people and their community/regional leaders and more fund for developments. This aspect gets revealed by the fact that, though a Union territory status was enough for region to attain and maintain its political identity from the neighbourhood, a statehood would give them power. Thus Manipur and Tripura in 1972, Mizoram and Arunachal Pradesh in 1986 and Goa in 1987 attained statehood from the status of the Union territory. Delhi achieved a special status among the Union territories in 1991. Its attainment of full statehood is a burning question now.

STATEHOOD AND POWER

➢ The Horizontal Problems of Statehood

Awareness about state autonomy has produced several political problems, both horizontal, that is, among the states and vertical, that is, between the Union and the states. In fringe areas and cities of most of the states live substantial population of linguistic (and religious) minorities. Their relations with the majority groups are not always happy. In some of the states of north-east India the inter-state borders contain rich forest resources on which the neighbours advance claims. Sharing of river water by states watered by big rivers have created enormous problems. Finally states reorganisation have occasionally changed the entire profile of a state creating revenue imbalance as in the case of Bihar after the separation of Jharkhand.

➢ The Union-State Relations Book Q.5

The issue of power haunts the Union-state relations in the country too. Roughly, this **problem may be treated** under the following rubrics:

1) Ideological-political: In 1959 the first communist state Government in India – Kerala – was superseded because of ideological incongruity with the Union Government. In 1967, when a number of state governments came into existence, the Union-state relations became extremely strained with rapid supersessions of the state Governments. In 1977, when the Janata Party replaced the Congress at the Union Government, governments in eight states were superseded by one stroke. In 1980, when the Congress returned to the Union government, eight Janata Party governments were dismissed at one stroke.

Gradually, however, as the single-party dominance came to end, and strong regional parties have come into existence. They tend to return to power through elections after their dismissal causing embarrassment to the Central Government. Parties have come to realise the futility of such power game. In 1993, in the Bommai case, the Supreme Court severely restricted the scope for such supersessions.

2) A related issue is what the states consider to be unnecessary intervention of the centre in the affairs of the states. Reservation of bills passed by the state legislatures by the Governors for the President's assent has created irritation among the states. In the late seventies the Union's decision to post its own security forces in the Union-run industries in the states created similar irritation.

3) But the most sustained conflict between the Union and the states relate to finance. The states' continuous and major complaint about the centre is that it has more money than it needs and more stingy about sharing its resources with the states than what is necessary.

Further, when the centre shares money with the states, it does so inequitably. **First,** there is a complaint that the centre is step-motherly about the Opposition-ruled states. **Second,** the principle of division of money among the states is not equitable. The rich states claim that, as they have developed faster than many other states and they contribute more revenue to the centre, their share in central allocations should be proportionate to their performance and contribution to the centre. The poor states claim that, as they have been victims of a long period of deprivation, their distress should be adequately remedied and they should be granted subsidies through higher allocation.

> ➤ **Constitutional Amendments** Book Q.6

Creation of new states and/or alteration of state boundaries, under Article 3 of the Constitution, do not require constitutional amendment as such. Whatever change is required to the provisions of the Constitution is effected through the Reorganisation Act itself. An exception was, however, made in the case of the large-scale reorganisation of states in 1956 when the seventh amendment to the Constitution was effected. It involved change of names of the states, transfer of territories, splits of existing Part A States, merger and split of Part B States, abolition of the categories of Part B and Part C States, conversion of Part D State of

Andaman and Nicobar Island into a Union territory, conversion of several Part C States into Union territories, redesigning of the administration of Union territories, reallocation of seats in the Council of States (Rajya Sabha) for the new states and certain related matters.

However, change in the Union-state relations has caused several amendments since 1954 (the Third Amendment Act). All these amendments, except the Forty-Second Amendment Act, were in the financial sphere. Though agriculture and industry other than defence industries

and industries declared to be of national importance was originally left in the states' sphere, the third amendment transferred trade and commerce in production, supply and distribution of the products of any industry and imported goods of the same kind where their control by the Union is declared by Parliament by law to be expedient to the public interest, food stuffs including edible oil seeds and oils, cattle fodder including oil cakes and other concentrates, raw cotton and cotton seed, and raw jute to concurrent jurisdiction of the centre and the states. By the sixth amendment (1956) the centre was given the power to tax sale and purchase of goods under inter-state trade and commerce. By the forty-sixth amendment (1982) the centre was given the power to tax sale and purchase under inter-state trade and commerce. These amendments indicated the expansive character of agriculture and animal husbandry requiring greater central intervention in their trade. The eightieth amendment in 2000, on the other hand, was the first attempt at forcing the centre to share with the states its enormous financial resources to an extent greater than before.

The Forty-Second Amendment Act (1976) effected a large number of changes in the Unionstate political relations. It enabled the Union Government to deploy any of its forces or any other force subject to its control or any of their units in any state in aid of civil power and control their powers, jurisdiction, privileges and liabilities (Para 2A of the Union List). It also transferred a number of state subjects to the Concurrent List, namely, education (Concurrent List 25), forest (Concurrent List 17A), Protection of wild animals and birds (Concurrent List 17B) and weights and measures except establishment of standards which was already in the Union List (Concurrent List 33A).

These trends indicate enhancement of the centre's power over the years. Yet one hears fewer complaints from the states about the centre's excessive power now except occasionally of a 'step-motherly treatment' of the Opposition-ruled states. The political balance has changed in favour of the states.

5.2: IGNOU Book Exercise – Solved

1) Trace the method of British annexation of India.

Answer by India Ebook: Answer is *marked* in 1 Shot Concept Above.

2) Trace the **evolving pattern of territorial arrangement** of India under the British.

Answer by India Ebook: Answer is *marked* in 1 Shot Concept Above.

3) How did the **Constituent Assembly** of India arrange the territory of independent India?

Answer by India Ebook: Answer is *marked* in 1 Shot Concept Above.

4) Trace the reorganisation of states in independent India. What are the consequential problems of the reorganisation on inter-state relations?

Answer by India Ebook: Answer is *marked* in 1 Shot Concept Above.

5) How is the Union-State relation evolving in India? What, according to you, are the main reasons for demand of state autonomy?

Answer by India Ebook: Answer is *marked* in 1 Shot Concept Above.

6) What are the Constitutional amendments which shaped the Union-State relations in India?

Answer by India Ebook: Answer is *marked* in 1 Shot Concept Above.

5.3: IGNOU Past 6 Attempts Question – Solved

Dec 2020: Write short note: (a) Constitutional mechanisms to resolve Inter-State disputes

Answer by India Ebook: Exact Same as Q.3 of Above.

June 2021: Discuss the changing nature of federalism in India.

Answer by India Ebook: Refer Marked Concept: Dynamics of Fedaralism.

June 2021: Write short not: (a) Constitutional amendments which shaped union-state relations in India.

Answer by India Ebook: Exact Same as Q.6 of Above.

6. ELECTIONS AND ELECTORAL POLITICS

Introduction
Role of Elections in Democracy
Election Machinery
Electoral System and Process
Election in India: An Exercise on Massive Scale
Voting Pattern
Determinants of Electoral Behaviour
Caste as a Determinant of Electoral Behaviour
Drawbacks of Electoral System
Electoral Reforms
> Change in the Electoral System
> Restructuring the Election Commission
> Eradicating the Evil Influences of Money and Muscle Power

6.1: One Shot Concepts

INTRODUCTION

Election is a device through which a modern state creates among its citizens a sense of involvement and participation in public affairs. A **good electoral system** is the *bedrock* of <u>genuine representative government</u>. Much depends on how the system operates in practice, whether competent and honest administrators free from political bias conduct elections efficiently and impartially. The absence of general confidence in the verdict of the ballot may destroy the faith of public in the democratic process.

India is a **constitutional democracy** with a *parliamentary system of government*, and at the heart of the system is a commitment to hold regular, free and fair elections. These elections determine the composition of the government, the membership of the two houses of parliament, the state and union territory legislative assemblies, and the Presidency and vicepresidency.

ROLE OF ELECTIONS IN DEMOCRACY Book Q.1

Nowadays, elections have emerged as an **instrument of choice** all over the democratic world. Elections serve as the basic mechanism for both electing and replacing ruling elites and for providing a regular and systematic succession in government. They help to determine how a country is governed and at the same time select who will exercise state power. Elections are also the principal mechanisms by which citizens hold governments accountable, both retrospectively for their policies and more generally for the manner in which they govern.

Although elections are considered as one of the core institutions in democratic polities, their misuse is not uncommon. Elections produce different outcomes in different systems of government. Military or civilian leaders willing to run the country through undemocratic means, use elections as a tool for their continuation in power. These leaders make major efforts to manipulate elections.

Electoral corruption is a major type of political corruption. It thrives in a society in which the degree of political and administrative morality is low. The necessity of a transparent electoral system is one of the most important prerequisites for present day democratic practice in both developed and developing countries. Electoral corruption negatively influences the consolidation of democracy. Governments, claiming to be democratic, manipulate elections to cling to power. Electoral malpractices are the main source of misunderstanding between the ruling and opposition parties in many states and have often led to political crisis. In India, Jammu and Kashmir is the classic example in this regard.

ELECTION MACHINERY   Book Q.1

Democratic practices are sustained and strengthened through elections. The authority vested with the conduct of elections should, therefore, be competent, effective, independent and impartial. The makers of the constitution of India had given the country an unified authority, **Election Commission (EC),** independent of the central and state governments, for organising elections to the Union and state legislatures. The powers of the EC are essentially administrative and marginally adjudicative and legislative. Its triple powers have so far been exercised without ever being objected to by the judiciary. It was initially envisaged to be a single member Commission. The EC was enlarged in October 1993 with the appointment of two ECs (Election Commissioners). The President appoints the CEC (Chief Election Commissioner) and ECs. The Tarkunde Committee in 1975 and the Goswami Committee in 1991 suggested that the President should make appointment to the EC on the advice of a Committee comprising the leader of the opposition in the Lok Sabha, the Prime Minister, and the Chief Justice of India.

ELECTORAL SYSTEM AND PROCESS

Elections are part of a larger political process, which includes nominations, campaigning, and the actual voting. In brief, all those means whereby a person becomes a member of an elected assembly can be termed as the electoral process. No developing countries can claim to meet these conditions fully. However, India comes closest to meeting them in comparison to others. It can rightly boast of an independent judiciary and a non-partisan election administration. Although India cannot claim to have a developed system of political parties, there is a general acceptance of certain rules of the game, which has gained deeper roots with time.

Elections have acquired a central place in the Indian political system. The campaigns are marked with intense political debates, symbolic processions and increasing use of electronic technology by major political parties. Visual symbols acquire greater importance in India due to widespread illiteracy. Voters identify the candidate with the help of the symbols allotted to them. Issues in form of slogans become critical at times like garibi hatao (remove poverty) in 1971, loktantra bachao (save democracy) in 1977, stable government in 1980, corruption in terms of Bofors scandal in 1989, mandal-mandir controversy in 1991.

ELECTION IN INDIA: AN EXERCISE ON MASSIVE SCALE

Elections are the great public ceremonies of Indian life. In India, the elections are massive spectacles mobilising millions of people into the political process. The elections tend to be complex events in India since they involve individual and collective decisions and directly affect the total political and social process. Unlike most of the new states in the developing countries, elections in India have been central, not peripheral to the system.

VOTING PATTERN

The General Election is considered as a sacred process that not only ratifies the principle of democracy generally but it strengthens the pillars of Indian democracy as well. The voting pattern shows that the percentage of female voters who cast their votes has significantly increased from 46.63 per cent in the third General Election to 55.64 per cent in 1999 election. A look at the results of the last five General Elections reveals that there is a decline in the performance of the national parties taken together both in terms of total number of seats won as well as their vote share. Regional parties gained at the cost of national parties during this period.

Elections are political processes, which provide a link between the society and the polity and between the traditional social systems and evolving political structures. Therefore, the elections must be analysed within the context of the total political and social system. Elections perform different roles in different political systems. They may contribute to political development in some, to political decay in others. They may sometimes be used as veiled disguises for authoritarianism.

In established democracies, there are institutional procedures for system maintenance and also the instruments for support building, interest aggregation, peaceful and orderly transfer of power, recruitment and training of leaders, and above all for an increasing democratisation of the political system. Thus, the elections are devices for legitimacy, identification, integration, communication, political education, participation, socialisation, mobilisation, conflict resolution, political choice, and political control. Elections induct an element of accountability into a political system and make it possible for the citizens to exercise a genuine and meaningful degree of political choice and control. This, in turn, makes the system itself a democratic and effective instrument of governance.

DRAWBACKS OF ELECTORAL SYSTEM   June 2020

The working of Indian electoral system has witnessed several drawbacks and malpractices. The discrepancy between the votes cast for a party and the seats won in parliament, the multiplicity of political parties, personality cult in party system, exploitation of caste and communal loyalties, role of muscle and money power, misuse of governmental machinery, fraudulent practices like booth-capturing, intimidation and impersonation of voters are important drawbacks of Indian electoral system.

Election malpractices range from the physical capturing of booths to the organisation of youth wings of parties or goon squads who could target and terrorise particular communities before the poll to prevent them from voting. Even the poll staff is either bribed into active connivance or intimidated into passive acquiescence. The menace of booth capturing has been in vogue since the second general election of 1957, especially in Bihar. The phenomenon gradually spread over the country in different forms and dimensions.

The rising need for the muscle power in elections necessitated more input of money too. Earlier voters used to be bribed individually, then it was found to be more convenient to buy musclemen who could ensure victory by capturing booth or intimidating voters rather than buying individual voters. This has led to progressive criminalisation of politics and the emergence of politician-underworld nexus. Gradually, the criminals themselves have started contesting elections instead of helping others. At times, the politicians found it necessary to politicise the bureaucracy. This can be gauged from the scale on which most of the high officials are changed with the change of a government.

6.2: IGNOU Book Exercise – Solved

1) Critically examine the role of election in democracy and evaluate the role of Election Commission of India in conducting free and fair poll.

Answer by India Ebook: Answer is *marked* in 1 Shot Concept Above.

2) What are the **important determinants** of electoral behaviour in India? Critically discuss the **role of caste as a determinant** of voting behaviour.

Answer by India Ebook: Election studies show that a combination of factors determines the **electoral behaviour**. These *factors include* mainly religion, language, region, caste, tribe, etc. In Punjab the religious, linguistic and regional factors have been used by the Akali Dal to garner votes. The regional and linguistic factors were used to mobilise votes in Tamil Nadu by the DMK, AIADMK, in Andhra Pradesh by the in Telugu Desam, in Assam by AGP. With increased democratisation and politicisation, the political parties have tried to exploit the caste factor for election purpose, which in turn enables elite group of castes to get inducted into the political process. In fact, caste is the most commonly used factor of mobilisatiom. It does, however, not mean that all the castes or even an entire caste becomes politicised or mobilised to influence the political system.

The **caste associations** in India began much before independence as agents of Sanskritisation seeking to secure educational, service and other facilities to raise the status of their caste in social hierarchy.

Caste has always played a decisive role in the **electoral politics** in India. While the higher caste Brahmins, Bhumihars, Rajputs have dominated the politics of several parts of India, the middle castes like Jats, Marathas, Yadvads, Reddies, Kammas, Vokkaliggas, etc., emerged powerful caste groups as a result of land reforms and Green Revolution. In the recent past even dalits, especially in North India have become an important and decisive caste group. The rise of the Bahujan Samaj Party in Uttar Pradesh is the most important example of increasing role of dalits. The caste groups, infact, have come to known as the "vote banks" of political parties in the light of their support to the parties.

Caste loyalties are to be exploited by the respective caste elites for their class interests. At the time of elections when it becomes more a question of number game, the caste groups seek to mobilise the support of not merely their own caste members but also those of others. Caste plays its role both in both ways - in the unorganised way and in the form of caste association caste. According to some scholars caste plays a secular role in Indian democracy. It has absorbed and synthesised some of the new democratic values, and has lost its ritual significance. In the democratic process caste affects the democracy and gets itself affected in turn.

3) What are electoral reforms? Discuss the various efforts made for electoral reforms.

Answer by India Ebook: The need of electoral reforms was felt quite early in India. The various committees and commissions appointed by the parliament, government and opposition parties have made attempts in this regard. First such major effort for electoral reforms was made in 1971, when a Joint Parliamentary Committee on Amendments to

Election Law was appointed under the chairmanship of Jagannath Rao, which submitted its report in 1972.

In 1974, Jayaprakash Narayan as president of the Citizens for Democracy (CFD) set up a committee under the chairmanship of Justice V.M. Tarkunde for electoral reforms. This committee popularly known as Tarkunde committee was asked to suggest measures to combat among other things the various forms of corrupt practice like the use of money and muscle power, misuse of official machinery and the disparity between the votes polled and the number of seats won, etc.

The Janata Party after assuming power in 1977 constituted a cabinet sub-committee on electoral reforms headed by the then Union Home Minister Charan Singh. At the same time, the CEC S.L. Shakdhar made significant suggestions on various issues ranging from election expenses to booth capturing. An agreement to reduce voting age from 21 to 18 years was also reached. But the Janata Party government fell before it could initiate any electoral reform.

The National Front government under V.P. Singh in January 1990 formed another committee on electoral reforms headed by the then Law Minister Dinesh Goswami. The committee did laudable and prompt work and submitted its report in May 1990. On the basis of the proposals therein, the government introduced four bills in the Parliament to give effect to its recommendations. But this government also fell before these bills could be enacted.

The Narasimha Rao government convened a special session of the Parliament to get two bills; the Constitution Eighty-Third Amendment Bill 1994 and the Representation of the People Second Amendment Bill, 1994, passed. However, the bills were withdrawn before introduction.

The United Front coalition government succeeded in getting the Representation of the People Second Amendment Act enacted in July 1996. The **important provisions** of the act are as follows:

i) Candidates will not be allowed to contest more than two seats at a time.

ii) Non-serious candidates will be deterred from contesting parliamentary and assembly elections through a ten-fold increase in the security deposit from Rs. 500 to Rs. 5000.

iii) Elections will not be countermanded because of the death of a candidate. In the case of a candidate of a recognised political party, the party will have the authority to nominate a replacement within seven days. No such replacement will be allowed in the case of an independent.

iv) The campaign period is **reduced from 21 days to 14 days.**

The reforms though minimal to begin with can pave the way for more through and comprehensive overhauling of the electoral machinery and process. The following measures can be suggested for electoral reform.

4) Explain the increasing role of money and muscle power in election. What measures can be adopted to curb its menace?

Answer by India Ebook: The working of Indian electoral system has witnessed several drawbacks and malpractices. The **rising need for the muscle power** in elections necessitated more input of money too. Earlier voters used to be bribed individually, then it was found to be more convenient to buy musclemen who could ensure victory by capturing booth or intimidating voters rather than buying individual voters. This has led to progressive criminalisation of politics and the emergence of politician-underworld nexus. Gradually, the criminals themselves have started contesting elections instead of helping others. At times, the politicians found it necessary to politicise the bureaucracy. This can be gauged from the scale on which most of the high officials are changed with the change of a government. This is done to condition the bureaucracy to act in favour of the ruling party during elections. The official machinery is used to collect information on political rivals. The official machinery come handy in hiring crowds, intimidating targeted sections of voters, creating local tensions, conditioning staff for poll duties, enrolling additional voters or removing certain names from there, etc.

To **check the increasing influence and vulgar show of money**, law should fix reasonable ceiling on election expenses and strict compliance of such law should be enforced as was done during T.N. Sheshan's tenure as the CEC. State funding of elections, which has been recommended by all the committees on electoral reforms, should be introduced to curb the menace of money in elections. To prevent growing criminalisation and violence there is an urgent need to implement the

EC's proposal of keeping out persons with proven criminal records from electoral context.

Model code of conduct should be enforced strictly. Gradually, ways and means must be found to implement the voters' right to recall as well as the right to reject candidates. The electoral process cannot be cleansed merely by legal measures. The electoral process is influenced and determined by the political culture of the political system, which cannot be reformed by legislative acts. The enlightened citizens who are prepared to uphold political norms and punish those who violates them can be an effective instrument for clean electoral politics.

Bolstering the intermediary political and civic institutions, whose collapse has accelerated electoral malpractices, can also be effective in removing the ills of electoral process. However, the strong political will and people's initiative is needed to get rid the electoral of from several defects from which it is suffering.

5) Explain the politician-underworld-bureaucracy nexus and its impact on the electoral process in India.

Answer by India Ebook: The **rising need for the muscle power** in elections necessitated more input of money too. Earlier voters used to be bribed individually, then it was found to be more convenient to buy musclemen who could ensure victory by capturing booth or intimidating voters rather than buying individual voters. This has led to progressive criminalisation of politics and the **emergence of politician-underworld nexus**. Gradually, the criminals themselves have started contesting elections instead of helping others. At times, the politicians found it necessary to politicise the bureaucracy. This can be gauged from the scale on which most of the high officials are changed with the change of a government. This is done to condition the bureaucracy to act in favour of the ruling party during elections. The official machinery is used to collect information on political rivals. The official machinery come handy in hiring crowds, intimidating targeted sections of voters, creating local tensions, conditioning staff for poll duties, enrolling additional voters or removing certain names from there, etc.

They also, in turn, allow the bureaucracy to make money so that they remain vulnerable. In the process significant sections of bureaucracy get incorporated into the politician-underworld-bureaucracy nexus. In its efforts to cleanse the electoral process, the EC has put a ban on transfers and promotions after the elections are announced. Although significant, the measure is of limited value as the final dispositions of the bureaucracy are usually made much in advance. Other practices of misuse have also been banned under model code of conduct that has come to be more strictly enforced since T.N. Seshan days.

Electioneering tends to be an expensive exercise. In a vast country like India this is more so because the electoral constituency is usually very large both in terms of size and population. With mass illiteracy, a candidate is required to make extensive personal contacts with the voters, which involve enormous expenditure. One important reason for the elections to have become so expensive in our times is the growing distance of political parties from the people. Transport, publicity and maintaining the campaigners involve enormous amount. The desire to win an election at any cost and the increasing reliance on the muscle power in elections have necessitated unbelievably enormous expenditures collected through dubious means, by the political parties and their candidates.

6.3: IGNOU Past 6 Attempts Question – Solved

June 2019: Write short note: (b) Election Commission

Answer by India Ebook: Almost same as **Q.1** above.

June 2020: Write short note: (b) Electoral malpractices in India

Answer by India Ebook: Refer Marked Concept: Drawback of Electoral Systems.

7. POLITICAL PARTIES AND PARTY SYSTEMS

7.1: One Shot Concepts

INTRODUCTION

Party system in a democracy normally refers to the pattern of interaction and competition between political parties. In India the pattern of interaction and competition among political parties has given way to the multi-party system. This kind of characterisation of the party system is, however, more accurate as of now than that existed a few decades ago. What existed then was the impeccable hegemony of the Congress Party and this was well characterised by Kothari and Jones as a 'dominant party system' that is a multiparty system, in which free competition among political parties occurred but it was the Indian National Congress which enjoyed a dominant position both in terms of the number of seats it held in the parliament and the state legislative assemblies, and in terms of its immense organisational strength. Kothari coined the term the 'Congress System' and Jones called it a 'Congress Dominated System'.

Enormous changes have taken place in the party system in recent years. These changes started taking place from 1967 onwards but these have become much more pronounced since the late eighties and early 1990s. The party system has moved away from a one party dominated

system to a multi-party system. It is also referred to as a federalised party system or a coalitional party system. This party system is marked by the presence of a dwindled Congress Party, a significant but inadequate growth of the **Bharatiya Janata Party (BJP)** and an enormous increase in the strength of the regional and state parties in national politics. We shall, in this unit, concern ourselves mainly with the party systems that had emerged and developed at the state level in the Indian union. But before doing so, we look at regional and state parties in brief since they have grown enormously in recent years and play a crucial role in shaping the party system in many of the Indian states.

REGIONAL AND STATE PARTIES

The **Election Commission** on regional parties is accepted widely in it is the academic circles, the Commission does not use the term regional parties. Instead it uses the term state parties. It classifies political parties into **three categories** — national, state and registered parties.

A party which is recognised as a state party in **four or more states** is a **national party**.

A party to be called a **state party** must have been engaged in political activity for at least 5 years and must have won either 4% of the seats in a general election or 3% in a state election. In addition it must have had the support of 6% of the votes cast.

A **registered party** is a party that is neither recognised as state or a national party but is registered with the Election Commission. Such parties are also termed as unrecognised parties.

The definition as provided by the **Election Commission** of a <u>regional party is not very satisfactory</u>. Since the definition takes into consideration the past performance of a political party, it is not accepted as a proper definition by the academicians. They consider those parties as regional parties whose bases and activities are restricted to a particular state and rooted in both regional aspirations and grievances. The support base of a regional party is limited to a particular state because it identifies itself with the region's culture, language, religion, etc. It also presents the regional perspective vis-à-vis the centre and other states. These parties use 'region' and 'language' effectively for electoral benefits.

There is a tendency among some scholars to include among the regional parties those parties which have an all India perspective but are confined to one state like the **Forward Bloc(FB)** in <u>**West Bengal**</u> or the **Workers' and Peasants' Party** in <u>**Maharashtra**</u>. The fundamental problem in this definition is that it does not take into consideration the ideology of parties. This definition takes into consideration only the social base of a party and its area of operation.

PARTY SYSTEM IN INDIAN STATES

State party systems in India have developed in close connection and interaction with the national party system. Closeness of relationships between the state party system and the national party system has been termed as the combination of the state party systems by some observers in the recent years. This is natural considering that India consists of different states. The changes in the national party system have affected the state party systems, and in turn transformation in the nature of party competition at the state level had affected the national party system substantially.

The second development, however, is more pronounced in recent years because of the spectacular growth of the regional and state parties in Indian politics. In this section we shall make an attempt to see the transformation that has taken place in the state party systems in the recent times.

> ### ➢ The Era of Congress Dominance   Book Q.2

The **party system** in India before **1967** has been as a system of Congress dominance. It has been also referred to as the "**Congress Dominated System**" or the "**Congress System**". Till the fourth general elections which were held in 1967 state party system in India, like that of the national party system, was dominated by the overwhelming presence of the Congress Party.

The Congress Party dominated in almost all the states. But the domination of congress was not uniform in all states. The Congress, for example, had to face the toughest competition in the former princely states that acceded to the Indian Union after 1947 whereas in other states it almost had an impeccable hegemony. It ruled almost all the states except Jammu and Kashmir where the National Conference had a domineering presence. Kerala was also an exception because in the second general elections in 1957, the CPI emerged victorious and formed a government along with its allies for two years till it was dissolved arbitrarily in 1959.

The Congress was such a dominant force that it secured comfortable majorities in almost all the elections to the Lok Sabha and the State Assemblies in 1952, 1957, 1962. Though it never secured more than 48 per cent of the votes in the Lok Sabha elections (the highest being 47.78 in 1957), it always secured comfortable majority in terms of seats (364 seats in 1952, 371 seats in 1957 and 361 in 1962). In the State assemblies, except for a few, it secured comfortable majorities almost in all the assembly elections. It secured 42.2 per cent of votes and 68.4 per cent of seats in 1952, 44.97 per cent of votes and 64.9 per cent of seats in 1957 and 43.65 per cent votes and 61.3 per cent of seats in 1962.

Let us briefly refer to this position of dominance across some of the bigger Indian states while referring to its performance in the assembly elections. In Uttar Pradesh assembly elections between 1952 and 1962, the party secured between 47.9 and 36.3 per cent votes. It captured between 390 to 249 seats, out of a total 430 seats. In Bihar, in the same period the party secured between 41.4 per cent to 42.1 per cent votes but between 72.2 per cent and 58.1 percent seats. Similarly, in West Bengal, the Congress secured between 38.9 and 47.3 per cent of votes and between 63 per cent to 62.3 per cent seats. In Andhra Pradesh, after the state was formed it secured between 41.7 per cent to 47.3 per cent votes in 1955-57 and 1962 and 187 to 177 seats (out of a total 300). In Tamil Nadu the party enjoyed a dominant position in the assembly elections of 1957 and 1962. It secured between 45.3 per cent and 46.1 per cent votes and captured between 67.4 per cent to 73.6 per cent seats. In Maharastra the party secured 48.7 per cent to 51.2 per cent of votes in 1952 and 1962. Thus it is clear that the Congress Party enjoyed a dominant position in the electoral politics of the states in the Indian Union, even though it was hardly able to secure the majority of the votes. In fact, it won a majority of seats in the assemblies of all the states on the basis of plurality of votes against a fragmented opposition.

> **The Breakdown of Congress System: 1967-1989**   June 2020

The **dominance** of the **Congress** in the states started **crumbling** from the **mid of 1960s**; the fourth general elections of 1967 marked the intensification of this change. The party system that emerged in the states after and continued till 1989 may be referred to as a bipolarised one in which a depleted Congress Party was confronted with a united opposition in most of the states. The following pattern of bipolarisation was seen in the states for the general elections in the period from 1967-1989. In Madhya Pradesh, Rajasthan, Himachal Pradesh and Delhi, the competition was between the Congress and the BJS/BJP. In Kerala,

Tripura and West Bengal the competition has been between the Congress and Left. In Punjab, Jammu and Kashmir, Andhra Pradesh, Assam and Goa, a Congress-regional parties led alliance emerged, though the BJP also gained substantially. In the North-Eastern states the contest was mainly between the Congress and a variety of regional parties or their alliances.

In Tamil Nadu, competition has been mainly between the DMK and the AIADMK. Finally in seven major states-Orissa, Maharashtra, Uttar Pradesh, Bihar, Haryana, Gujarat and Karnataka-the Congress retained preponderance. One can, however, add that even in these states opposition grew stronger as we shall notice later. So far as the assembly elections are concerned, the following pattern of bipolarisation emerged after 1967. One may note that the votes of the Congress party declined much more drastically in the assembly elections than in the parliamentary ones. In Madhya Pradesh, Rajasthan, Himachal Pradesh and Delhi, the non-Congress votes consolidated in favour of the BJS/BJP. Finally, in the seven states — Uttar Pradesh, Orissa, Bihar, Haryana, Gujarat, Maharashtra and Karnataka Congress remained almost dominant.

Let us have a look at how these changes occurred. We shall refer mainly to the party systems that we witness in the state assembly elections. It has been noted earlier that the Congress had never secured more than 50 per cent of the votes either in the parliamentary or assembly elections except in some states but has always secured huge majorities in terms of seats. This is indicative of the fact that though significant opposition to the Congress existed at the state level due to fragmentation in their ranks and because of the rule associated with the "first past the post system," the Congress always emerged victorious in terms of seats. The 1967 election in fact put an end, at least for a temporary period, to this disunity in the opposition. The post-1967 period saw the emergence of anti-Congress alliances in state after state and this altered the nature of the contests particularly for the assemblies. These developments resulted in the defeat of the Congress in as many as eight out of sixteen states of the Indian Union. There was also a marked decline in the vote share of the Congress party in the parliamentary elections from 44.72 in 1962 to 40.7 per cent in 1967.

We also note that in the early 1970s the Congress was able to make a comeback after 1972 for a brief period. This position was soon lost by the party in the late 1970s. In the West, in Maharashtra, strong challenge to Congress hegemony came in 1978 and later from the mid of the 1980s. In the 1978 assembly elections the Congress led by Indira Gandhi was routed. In central India, in Madhya Pradesh, the largest of the Indian states, the Congress was challenged by the BJS/BJP in 1972, 1980 and 1985. It was challenged by the Janata Party in 1977. The BJS secured 28.7 per cent votes in 1980, the BJP secured 30.3 per cent and in 1985 it could secure 32.4 per cent votes.

TOWARDS FRAGMENTATION OF STATE PARTY SYSTEMS: 1989 ONWARDS
Book Q.3

At the national level there has been an end of the one party dominance and the movement towards a multi-party system; as you have read earlier this trend started in 1967 at the state level. However, the systems that exist in the states are different from the national level. Many states have moved towards a two party system and probably this is the most prominent feature of party competition at the state level.

At the national level in recent years competition has narrowed down to two different alliances, one led by the BJP and the other by the Congress. The 'Third Front' has petered out. At the state level the nature of competition differs. The competing parties differ from state to state but in most of the states it is a two party system. In many states it is a multi-party system where the important contenders are the Congress, the BJP and state or regional parties.

The Congress Party had started declining since the late 1960s in the states but this decline became much more prominent in the late 1980s. We have seen earlier that the Congress that had enjoyed dominance at the state level for more than two decades gradually started declining after the death of Nehru. The decline of Congress became more spectacular after Indira Gandhi assumed the leadership of the party. There are numerous explanations for this.

The **expansion** of the **BJP** in recent times has been much **more dramatic** than the decline of the Congress. The expansion has mainly been due to the decline of the Congress, the aggressive mobilisation strategy based around the **ideology of Hindutva** which it adopted from the late **1980s** and its strategy of alliance formation. At the national level in the Lok Sabha, it increased its seats from a 2 in 1984 to 182 seats in the 1998 elections that catapulted it to the position of a ruling party. In 1999 it secured the same number of seats, though, along with its allies, it was able to consolidate its position as a ruling party. However, this onward march of the BJP was halted in the 2004 general elections.

It is due to these interrelated developments that the party systems in the states had undergone significant transformation in recent years more particularly from 1989 onwards. From a system that was Congress—dominated (like that of the national party system) it has become fragmented. In this fragmented system, the competition is primarily between two parties whether national or regional but — there are others who occupy a significant position in the party politics of the states.

To the **first category** belong states like Himachal Pradesh, Madhya Pradesh, Rajasthan and Gujarat. These states are essentially two party states in terms of vote and seat share. Included in this category are West Bengal, Kerala, Tripura, Maharastra and Punjab which are essentially bipolar states. In these states either two alliances or one-party opposed by an alliance of two or smaller parties dominate party politics.

In the **second category** belongs to those states like Karnataka, Bihar and Orissa where there are three or more poles though it appears that in future it will drift towards a bipolar system either due to alliances or due to splits in existing parties.

Thirdly, there are states like Uttar Pradesh where a four-cornered contest exists between the BJP, Samajwadi Party, the Bahujan Samaj Party and the Indian National Congress.

The **fourth category** belongs to those states in which a bipolar or two-party system exists but there is also an increasing growth of a third party. The third party may not be strong enough to capture large number of seats but has a significant vote share.

7.2: IGNOU Book Exercise – Solved

1) State party systems in India have developed in close connection and interaction with the national party system. Discuss.

Answer by India Ebook: State party systems in India have developed in close connection and interaction with the national party system. Closeness of relationships between the state party system and the national party system has been termed as the combination of the state party systems by some observers in the recent years. This is natural considering that India consists of different states. The changes in the national party system have affected the state party systems, and in turn transformation in the nature of party competition at the state level had affected the national party system substantially.

The second development, however, is more pronounced in recent years because of the spectacular growth of the regional and state parties in Indian politics. In this section we shall make an attempt to see the transformation that has taken place in the state party systems in the recent times.

The Election Commission on regional parties is accepted widely in it is the academic circles, the Commission does not use the term regional parties. Instead it uses the term state parties. It classifies political parties into three categories — national, state and registered parties.

A party which is recognised as a state party in four or more states is a national party.

A party to be called a state party must have been engaged in political activity for at least 5 years and must have won either 4% of the seats in a general election or 3% in a state election. In addition it must have had the support of 6% of the votes cast.

A registered party is a party that is neither recognised as state or a national party but is registered with the Election Commission. Such parties are also termed as unrecognised parties.

The definition as provided by the Election Commission of a regional party is not very satisfactory.

2) Briefly analyse the era of Congress dominance.

Answer by India Ebook: Refer the Marked 1 Shot Concept Above.

3) Examine the developments towards the multiparty system in India. Give an example.

Answer by India Ebook: Refer the Marked 1 Shot Concept Above.

7.3: IGNOU Past 6 Attempts Question - Solved

June 2019: Examine the major changes in the party systems in the states since the late 1960s.

Dec 2021: Analyse the changes in the pattern of State politics in India since the 1960s.

Answer by India Ebook: **Almost Same as Q.2 Above.**

June 2020: Examine the factors contributing to the breakdown of the Congress system.

Answer by India Ebook: See Marked Concept.

Dec 2020: Examine the factors leading to the fragmentation of party system in India.

June 2021: Examine the development leading to fragmentation of state party systems in India.

Answer by India Ebook: Same as **Q.3** above.

8. PATTERNS OF DISSENT AND PROTEST MOVEMENTS IN INDIAN STATES

Introduction
Meanings: Dissent and Protest
Protest Movements and Social Movements
Characteristics and Patterns of Protest Movements
Examples of Protest Movements
- ➢ The Naxalite Movements
- ➢ The Chhattisgarh Mukti Morcha (CMM)
- ➢ The Self-Determination Movements
- ➢ Anti-Development Movements

8.1: One Shot Concepts

INTRODUCTION

A large number of people are not satisfied with the existing pattern of relations. They find the economic, social, cultural and political aspects of these relations unjust and one-sided. People have protested in different states of India against such patterns of relations. The protest of people have taken the form of protest movements.

MEANINGS: DISSENT AND PROTEST

The history of human civilisation is marked by "dissents" and "protests" within human relationships and human groups and also between civil and political society. **Dissent** means disagreement or withholding assent. It has a negative connotation i.e. a dissenter is a non-conformist. During medieval period dissent was considered as sacrilege. However, in democracy it acquired a new meaning carrying the notion of radical and hence not conforming to the values that are either "authoritatively" allocated by the state or practiced by the civil society. **Protest is something more than dissent**. It emerges out from dissent and is a concrete form or expression of disapproval or objection.

Protest and dissent are **inseparable** so much so that without dissent protest does not have any meaning. If both dissent and protest form the basis of human organisation into a group and with its own goal, leadership, certain degree of motivation and political communication, it takes the shape of a movement. Movements entail collective action to transform and change the status quo. In a democratic society, such kinds of movements are referred to as "social movements" in general and since the later part of the twentieth century as "new social movements".

These movements build upon various themes such as ecology, gender, human rights and so on, present a kind of pattern that requires incisive analysis. The protest is expressed against any form of domination and discrimination. The protest movements are movements against unjust and unequal order in social, economic, political or cultural form.

PROTEST MOVEMENTS AND SOCIAL MOVEMENTS

The **Protest Movements** are meant to change the patterns of relations in the social domain, and the **Social Movements** are related to political aspects. But some scholars like **Ghanshyam Shah** argue that there is no difference between social and political movements; both are used synonymously. The components of a social movement are the ideology, programmes, strategy, objectives of social change leadership and patterns of mobilisation. Social movements are usually specific to culture, history and social structure. Issues and strategies of movements are relative to societies and to their history. For instance, quest for freedom may become the central issue for the struggle of a collectivity in one society, in one period; the same quest may emerge in another society in another period. The mission in the movements is to reject or alter the past and present forms of norms and values of society to have a better society.

The **state perceives** the protest and social movements as a **challenge** to its legitimacy of governance. So the immediate response of the State is negative and suppressive. If the intensity of the movements is high, the state uses various strategies and tactics to diffuse collective action by soft paddling and leniency involving dialogue and negotiation and appeasing and co-opting the participants.

Ghanshyam Shah classifies movements into **revolt, rebellion, reform** and **revolution** to bring about changes in the political system. **Reform** seeks to change in the part of the system and does not challenge the political system per se; **revolt** poses a challenge to political authority, aiming at overthrowing the government; **rebellion** aims at attacking the existing authority without any intention to seize state power and in **revolution**, a section or sections of the society launch an organised struggle to overthrow not only the established government and regime but also socio-economic structure which sustains it, and replace the structure by an alternative social order.

M.S.A. Rao also offers a typology that movements as reformist, transformatory and revolutionary. **David Baylely** divides 'coercive public protest' into legal and illegal protest further, each category subdivided into violent and non-violent protests. Another classification may be grassroots and macro movements, or on the basis of issues around which participants get mobilised.

CHARACTERISTICS AND PATTERNS OF PROTEST MOVEMENTS   June 2021

There has been a spurt of protest movements since the 1970s in different states of India. These movements have been identified as the new social movements by some scholars. They are new in the sense that they have emerged in new context, Gail Omvedt identifies the main characteristic of these movements as apolitical, with new organisation and leadership aiming to change the relations of dominance and subordination. But all protest movements can not be termed as new social movements, since they still raise the issues which are related to the traditional economic and social relations.

In almost all states of India there are some **characteristics and patterns** of protest movements. The **principal patterns** can be identified as follows:

1) Disenchantment with the formal political institutions,

2) Increased violence within the civil society

3) Failure of state to deliver public good and services

4) Emergence of new social and political forces, and

5) States' response in the form of coercion, accommodation and repression

Mass movements or protests are largely have got subsumed in the popular culture being promoted as the 'globalised culture'. The Marxist scholars attribute it to the 'multilineal character' and 'all pervasive hierarchy' of the Indian society. However, some scholars criticise this and say that the protest movements are the result of the clash between 'tradition' and 'modernity'. The revolution of rising expectations of people is not met with political justice and hence there emerges a gap between 'political instability' and 'disorder'.

EXAMPLES OF PROTEST MOVEMENTS

There are large number cases of dissent and protest movements in several states of India. These movements include those of all sections society. Some of these want to change the pattern dominance and subordination; some want to reinforce their dominance by demanding more concessions from the state; some challenge even the notion of nation-state.

➢ **The Naxalite Movements** Book Q.2

Different shades of naxalite movements express protest against three sources of exploitation i.e. the unequal and exploitative economic relations, the oppressive caste system and the Indian states. According to them the exploiting classes in collaboration with imperialist forces and using the feudal-capitalist ideologies exploit the poor people. The solution to the problem lies in overthrowing the existing political, social and economic system. They profess the use of violent means in achieving their goal. The naxalites have been against participating in elections. But some of them have changed their attitudes about elections and have participated the elections.

The naxalite movement, which started by Kanu Sanyal and Charu Mazumdar in Naxalbari area of West Bengal in 1967 spread into several states in some years. The principal states among these are Andhra Pradesh, Bihar, Jharkhand, Chhattisgarh, Orissa, Punjab and Uttar Pradesh.

But naxalites do not have wide spread social base in these states. They have strong pockets of support there. The main naxalite organisations are Bihar Pradesh Kisan Sabha (BPKs), the Marxist Coordination Committee (MCC) and the People's War Group. The naxalites have mobilised people on issues like increase in agricultural wages, land to the tiller. In Bihar, particularly, they have combined their struggle against class discrimination with the steuggle against caste oppression. They have targeted their class enemies with violence, including kidnapping.

➢ **The Chhattisgarh Mukti Morcha (CMM)** Book Q.3

Chhattisgarh, a region in Madhya Pradesh till 2000, and thereafter a state, is more known by its liberation front (Chhattisgarh Mukti Morcha), a protest movement exposing the interface between governance and civil society, than by anything else. This movement informs us that the relationship between some sections of civil society and the government is not always reciprocal or complementary, and that it may well be conflictual. The deep fault lies within civil society, which exists between dominant and subaltern groups. Society is deeply conflictive and hierarchically organised sphere, wherein the "haves" - rich and upper caste groups – form the social basis of the State, while the other groups – "have-nots" – are oppressed both by the state and the dominant groups. It is this oppressed group which protests and challenges both sets of interest i.e. the interest of the dominant group and the state – in the form of a "social movement".

The struggle of the workers in Chhattisgarh is rooted in the development and modernising project that denies them their basic rights and exploits them with pain and misery. It was with the establishment of the Bhilai Steel Plant (BSP) that new development took place in the socioeconomic arena. The plant recruited only 10 per cent of the total 70,000 workers who were asked to perform casual manual work under hazardous conditions. The payment of wages to the daily casual workforce was erratic and much below the prescribed minimum wage.

With the formation of CMM, the domain of the struggle expanded and by 1990s, it had developed into a well-organised trade union. However, in its initial formation stage it marked the culmination of a struggle that had recognised that any movement for workers needs to integrate both their living and working conditions.

> **The Self-Determination Movements**   Book Q.4 Part1

Self-determination movements express dissent against the existing arrangement of relations between the principal political unit and its constituent units. In relation to the nation-state, certain nationalities, and in relation to the dominant nationalities the smaller nationalities question the existing relations. They feel that such an arrangement was unjust and detrimental to their interests.

On the contrary it favoured the dominant groups. In order to change this type of relations, the smaller nationalities start self-determination movements. Such movements may assume the form of autonomy movements demanding separate political unit from the existing dominant unit with due respect to the sovereignty of nation-state. They may also question the sovereignty of the nation-state and demand establishment of their own sovereign state. Various states in India have witnessed the rise and fall different forms of self-determination movements at different point of times. The principal examples of demands in various states for the formation of separate states within the parameters of Indian constitution include the formation of Telangana state, Vidharbha, Harit Pradesh, etc. Recently in 2002 three new states were created as a result of movements which demand their formation. These states are Uttaranchal, Chhattisgarh and Jharkhand. The demand for creation of sovereign states has come mainly from the North-East, Jammu and Kashmir and Punjab. Earlier such demand was made in the Tamil speaking areas of south India. It is important to note here that all self-determination movements in these regions do not advocate sovereign state for them; they would like to have a suitable rearrangement of federal relations within the framework of Indian constitution.

> ## Anti-Development Movements   Book Q.4 Part2

Development based on the modern scientific approaches has not been sustainable. It means that for the development - setting up modern institutions, industries, dams etc., the natural resources have been used in such a way that they can not be retained. Apart from the depletion of natural resources, development has also caused miseries to human being. On the one had it has led to the displacement and migration of people from their traditional habitat, on the other hand their traditional knowledge has been made redundant. People - the civil society, NGOs, grass root organisations, have responded to the encroachment by development and modernisation in different fields- against construction of big dams, deforestation, etc. They have demanded that development should be sustainable; it means that the natural resources and traditional knowledge should be used in such way that natural resources are not totally depleted and the traditional knowledge is retained. Such development is known as sustainable. There has been reaction for and against development. It is opposed by the people who feel adversely affected, by intellectuals, Gandhians, NGOs sympathetic to the affected people, and by the states where the affected people reside. Conversely, industrialists, the foreign funding agencies like World Bank and IMF extend their support to such development. Most important examples of

Peoples' protest against development include Narmada Bachao Andolan and the environmental movements. Narmada Bachao Andolan which has continued for more than three decades in different forms has got strong opposition and support. The construction of Sardar Sarovar Dam, which is opposed by the **Narmada Bachoa Andolan** is supported by different Gujarat governments, politicians, and the World Bank, but it has been opposed by Narmada Bachao Andolan, people, politicians and governments in Madhya Pradesh and Chhattishgarh. The attitude of the central government has been ambivalent dictated by the political considerations.

8.2: IGNOU Book Exercise – Solved

1) Discuss the relationships between the social movements and protest movements.

Answer by India Ebook: The protest movements are forms of social movements. The former are meant to change the patterns of relations in the social domain, and the latter are related to political aspects. But some scholars like Ghanshyam Shah argue that there is no difference between social and political movements; both are used synonymously. The study of social movements seeks to focus on political sociology, that is, the study of politics of the masses, their aspirations and demands, articulation of their problems, the modus operandi in asserting their demands outside the institutional framework and their occasional efforts at overthrowing the existing state power. Political scientists had largely ignored this area of study for greater understanding of political processes. The recent emphasis on social movements indicates a marked shift from positivism, institutionalism, constitutionalism and state-centricism perspectives towards a holistic understanding of social conflict and change.

The components of a social movement are the ideology, programmes, strategy, objectives of social change leadership and patterns of mobilisation. Social movements are usually specific to culture, history and social structure. Issues and strategies of movements are relative to societies and to their history. For instance, quest for freedom may become the central issue for the struggle of a collectivity in one society, in one period; the same quest may emerge in another society in another period. The mission in the movements is to reject or alter the past and present forms of norms and values of society to have a better society. The idea of 'social transformation' or 'change' is at the core of social optimism, and therefore, challenges the fixed notions of values, norms, power and hierarchy in the society. It aims for social optimism by 'deconstructing' the critical conflictual aspects.

There have been protest movements in different states of India. These protest have been against the real or perceived discrimination or unequal social, economic, cultural or political relations. Protest movements also form some kind of social movements. In Indian states there have been various kinds of protest movements. Different shades of Naxalite movements, Chhattisgarh Mukti Morcha, self-determination movements and anti-development movements, which have been discussed provide an understanding to the patterns of dissent protest in India states.

2) Write a note on the Naxalite movements.

Answer by India Ebook: Read the 1 Shot Concept Above.

3) Analyse the Chhattisgargh Mukti Morcha.

Answer by India Ebook: Read the 1 Shot Concept Above.

4) Compare the self-determination movements and anti-development movements.

Answer by India Ebook: Read the 1 Shot Concept Above.

8.3: IGNOU Past 6 Attempts Question – Solved

June 2021: Comment on the nature and pattern of protest movements in India.

Answer by India Ebook: See Marked Concept: Characteristics and Patterns of Protest Movements.

9. DEVELOPMENTAL ISSUES AND REGIONAL DESPARITIES

Introduction

Meanings of Development

- ➢ Western Meaning
- ➢ Development as Underdevelopment
- ➢ Development as Freedom
- ➢ Development as Sustainable Development

Development as Regional Disparities

- ➢ Diversity as the Cause of Regional Disparities
- ➢ Historical Advantages
- ➢ Diseconomies of Scale verses Agglomeration Advantages and Regional Disparities

Development and Regional Disparities in India

- ➢ The Colonial Impact
- ➢ Level of Regional Disparities in Human Development

9.1: One Shot Concepts

INTRODUCTION

Development emerged as an overarching and ensemble concept in the twentieth century and it was considered the rationality and legality of the age. But today, there are very few who accept it uncritically and without reservations. It is worth noticing that more often than not development was used to serve vested interest as every dominant group tried to interpret it to justify its ends. Consequently at the end of a long saga of narratives and discourses development emerged as a protean concept meaning different things to different people.

For example development that promised freedom and emancipation from all types of tyrannies for all, in its inception had become inimical to human freedom at the end of the last century. In between these two extremes development changed its meanings many times serving different purposes ranging from the reason of the state, legitimiser of the regimes, as component of vision of a good society and above all, as shorthand terms for the needs of the poor and needy.

MEANINGS OF DEVELOPMENT

Development means different things to different people. Similarly issues of development have varied according to the meanings of development. In this sub-section you will study about the developmental issues according to different meanings of development.

➤ Western Meaning

During the age of the Empires development meant discovery of new territories in search of market for their finished products and raw materials for their industries and their subsequent colonisation. It also meant spread and imposition of the European culture, civilisation and political power over other communities in other parts of the world. In achieving these goals they used both temptation as well as brute force. But as far as the colonies are concerned this was the beginning of the age of degradation, distortion and dependent development.

Hereafter development symbolised the plunder and plight of the people in the colonies. This process continued till the end of World War II when some new meanings and interpenetrations were assigned to the concept 'development'. An important dimension of these new meanings and interpretations was the realisation of the need for the generation of data on the per capita real income as the basis for distinguishing developed countries from the underdeveloped ones. The **following factors were identified** by a committee for asserting the low level of development in the developing committies:

☐ Apparent lack of desire within the poor nations for material wealth and entrepreneurship;

☐ Poor system of governance and law;

☐ Low levels of literacy; and

☐ Inhospitable culture for development etc. is responsible for low levels of development in the developing countries.

➤ Development as Underdevelopment

The aggressive approach adopted by the western powers particularly the United States of America and its Brettonwood institutions like the **World Bank** (WB) and the **International Monetary Funds** (IMF) towards the development did not go unchallenged. Though these western powers graduated from strong to stronger positions under the cold war and they also pontificated their success stories of development for peace world over, yet there emerged some theoreticians who championed the cause of the victims of the aggressive Pax Economica/Pax Americana.

As a result of all these the world got divided into **two** diametrical opposite poles i.e. **the developed** and the **underdeveloped world**. Though these are distinct in the characteristics, yet both share common historical experience and emanate from the one and the same processes. Some of the **important characteristics** of an **underdeveloped economy** are as follows:

1) Transition to Peripheral Capitalism: Most of the colonies in the tropical, subtropical and equatorial areas were subjected to specialisation in the export of primary products. Most of the products included in this category were related agriculture and mining activities.

2) Extraversionism: Though the colonies specialised in the production of the primary and semi-processed goods in the secondary sector, these products had limited demands in the domestic market. Large share of these products were produced to meet the external demands. Thus, the colonial economy was always regulated through the forces of world market.

3) Hpertrophism: It was imperative on the part of the mother country to create institutions in the colonies for the purpose of governance and uninterrupted supply of raw material and distribution of the finished products. Disproportionate growth of tertiary sector was done to achieve this objective. Subsequently service sector constituted the second highest share of employment after agriculture in the colonies. This resulted in the tertiarisation of the colonial economy and society.

> **Development as Freedom**

Twentieth century has been one of the most eventful times in human history. Humanity experienced rising hopes and abysmal despairs and dejections at one and the same time. It underwent a series of revolutionary as well as counter-revolutionary changes with in a short span of time. Science opened new vistas of possibilities in human endeavour but at the same time some of its inventions placed human destiny in a state of utter helplessness and desperations. We are faced with scientific as well as religious fundamentalism. In a nut shell, our balance sheet of gains and loses become a matter of interpretations and positions. However, there are at least two clear agendas that emerged out of the upheavals of the last century.

Astronomic rise in secular uncertainties is the first and most important out come. Today the developed as well as the underdeveloped worlds are gripped in the fear of uncertainties and risks. This is possibly one of the reasons that both science and religion have adopted aggressive positions as both accept use of force as legitimate means to assert ones claims.

Secondly, freedom has emerged as the minimum condition for the existence of every one. Freedom is considered one's ontological necessity and a birthright. People are ready to pay any price for their freedom. It is considered a minimum condition for one's social and individual survival.

In another words economic development alone does not guarantee freedom and democracy. On the contrary, removal of poverty and providing adequate public facilities, social care, organisational arrangements for health care particularly epidemiological programmes; education facilities and effective institutions for the maintenance of local peace and order etc. are the other essential requirement for the success of both democracy and development. He also established deep inter-connections between freedom and development for two reasons:

☐ **Evaluative reasons:** the assessment of development has to be done in terms of whether the freedom people have is increasing; and

☐ **Effective reason:** whether the freedom people enjoy is reinforced and guaranteed through a sustainable agency.

Thus, development and freedom find new meanings in his formulations.

> **Development as Sustainable Development**

Development, which has been claimed by different scholars as indispensable particularly for world peace, freedom, democracy and modernisation etc. belied all these claims. On the contrary, it symbolised ever increasing social inequalities, regional disparities, displacement of people and spread of disease and hunger globally, apart from putting humanity on the path of a long war against the environment and cultural pluralities. Therefore, a new set of scholars questioned the entire process and concept of development. They criticised the scholars from the underdeveloped school for their lop-sided treatment of development. Recently there has been inclusion of some more issues in the ongoing process of development which has been criticised from one more angle.

The most significant of these issues are related to environmental degradation, ecological crises and socio-ecological disasters.

The decade of the 1980s as also significant in the history of development because so far most of the critiques of development were made by the individuals at the local or regional levels but hereafter it came to be realised at the world level that the cost of development is increasingly out weighing its advantages. **Ecological disasters** like global warming, ozone layer depletion, emission of nuclear radiation and other types of pollutions have crossed the tolerance limits and if unchecked the future of humanity itself is at stake. It was felt imperative that so far development and its critiques have taken into consideration only human well beings and they have turned a blind eyes to other partners in the entire development process namely the environment. First major and concerted efforts at the Global level was made after constituting a **Commission on Global Environment** under the auspices of the **United Nations** popularly known as **Stockholm Conference on Environment**.

The proceedings of the conference were subsequently published in reports entitled "the **Brundtland Commission Report**" and also "**Our Common Future**". It is from this conference that the concept Sustainable Development got its currency and was accepted as the most fundamental contribution to overcome the crises that were created by the ongoing development. The gist of the concept **'Sustainable development'** in the report was in these words: "Development that meets the needs of the present without compromising the abilities of the future generations to meet their own need, improved living standard for all, better protected and managed ecosystem and a safer, more prosperous future".

DEVELOPMENT AS REGIONAL DISPARITIES

The experiences of the ongoing development activities at the local, regional, national and global levels suggest that development is essentially a differentiating activity. Scholars have suggested in the past that development in its initial stages results into regional and social divergences, it creates imbalance and inequalities but over a longer period of time these inequalities get reduced. Some of the factors responsible for the divergence convergence processes of development are:

> ### Diversity as the Cause of Regional Disparities

It is argued that there are regions that enjoy certain relative advantages over others in terms of their natural resource endowments. Apart from these the relative advantages may also include rich resource base, favourable climatic conditions and easy accessibility in terms of its geographical location etc. It is agued that over time the relative advantages enjoyed by the developed region will reach a saturation point and there after it will remain no more lucrative and profiteering for the entrepreneurs to continue in their usual ways by restricting enterprises to developed regions only. On the contrary, they will have to move towards the backward regions in search of market, resources, labour force and investment opportunities etc. This will increase the interaction between the developed and the backward regions and consequently the backward regions will also benefit from these changes and ultimately succeed in bridging the gap and balanced development will be a possibility.

> ### Historical Advantages

It is believed that the division of the world into developed and underdeveloped parts or core and periphery is largely due to the historical processes which were set into motion with the onset of modern world system and capitalism. It is largely due to the replication of the capitalist structure at different levels that different regions have performed differently as far as their development is concern. There are not only developed core and backward peripheries at the global levels but also developed regions and backward peripheries with in the backward region and the structure continuously gets reproduced at subsequently levels. The legacy of colonial rule and particularly the regional and structural distortions that were introduced by the coloniser is largely responsible for inter and intra regional disparities in the colonies.

> ### Diseconomies of Scale verses Agglomeration Advantages and Regional Disparities

An entrepreneur always moves from regions of lower to higher economic opportunities. Economic opportunities may be in the form of rich resource base, ideal social and political climate, better accessibilities to market and raw material sources but it can also be in the form of availing certain agglomeration advantages.

There are scholars who believe that **lack** of *capital resources* and rate of *technological innovations*, their diffusions and gestation period etc. contribute in the development as well as backwardness of a region. Regions that show positive performance towards these indicators develop faster than those are slow in their response. Differences in these, result into consolidation of regional disparities. There are some scholars who believe that lack of enthusiasm among certain culture groups regarding the use of modern technology and their reluctance to venturing into new enterprises has depressing impacts on the development impetus among some countries. As a result they remain at the low level of development. **India is a classic case** of the <u>**paradox of development and disparity**</u>.

DEVELOPMENT AND REGIONAL DISPARITIES IN INDIA

➢ Colonial Impact

India has a long history of colonialism, the foreign domination and experiencing dependent development. Owing to its precarious position within the British colonial power it was subjected to colonial exploitation as well as disarticulations in its economic, social and regional structures. Uneven development was deeply entrenched into the very process of social formation and its remedy also lay in the structural transformation. Though India fought a prolonged struggle against the colonial domination, yet it also avoided addressing the issue of structural transformation.

Consequently nothing much was expected after the independence of the country. In place of taking such a radical step India pursued a path of mixed economic development. This resulted into further consolidation of regional disparities and uneven development. Though regional disparities are pervasive and they are well pronounced in every aspects of our social life, yet the most significant articulation of these is found in the process and level of human development in India. Regional disparities in Human development epitomises the totality of social inequalities and regional disparities in India.

➢ Levels of Regional Disparities in Human Development

Welfare and well-being of its citizens is the sole aim of development in any country. Human development is "a process of enlarging the range of peoples choices- increasing their opportunities for education, health care, income and employment and covering the full range of human choices from a sound physical environment to economic and political freedom". Thus human development constitutes the core of every development project. Though most of the countries including India remain committed to this aim irrespective of differences in their approaches to achieve the desired objectives, yet the real issue of human development continues to remain a matter of intrigue as far as its translation into practice is concern. There are certain regions which show high levels of human development while there are others that occupy the last position in the scale of development. India is a classical example in this respect.

9.2: IGNOU Book Exercise – Solved

1) Identify the major developmental issues according to different meanings of development.

Answer by India Ebook: Development means different things to different people. Similarly issues of development have varied according to the meanings of development. During the **age of the Empires** development meant discovery of new territories in search of market for their finished products and raw materials for their industries and their subsequent colonisation. It also meant spread and imposition of the European culture, civilisation and political power over other communities in other parts of the world.

The aggressive approach adopted by the **western powers** particularly the United States of America **(USA)** and its **Brettonwood** institutions like the **World Bank** (WB) and the **International Monetary Funds** (IMF) towards the development did not go unchallenged. Though these western powers graduated from strong to stronger positions under the cold war and they also pontificated their success stories of development for peace world over, yet there emerged some theoreticians who championed the cause of the victims of the aggressive Pax Economica/Pax Americana.

Economic development alone does not guarantee **freedom and democracy.** As a result of all these the world got divided into two diametrical opposite poles i.e. the developed and the underdeveloped world. On the contrary, removal of poverty and providing adequate public facilities, social care, organisational arrangements for health care particularly epidemiological programmes; education facilities and effective institutions for the maintenance of local peace and order etc. are the other essential requirement for the success of both democracy and development.

Development, which has been claimed by different scholars as indispensable particularly for world peace, freedom, democracy and modernisation etc. belied all these claims. On the contrary, it symbolised ever increasing social inequalities, regional disparities, displacement of people and spread of disease and hunger globally, apart from putting humanity on the path of a long war against the environment and cultural pluralities. Therefore, a new set of scholars questioned the entire process and concept of development. The most significant of these issues are related to environmental degradation, ecological crises and socio-ecological disasters.

2) What conclusions do you draw about regional disparities in India?

Answer by India Ebook: There are some scholars who believe that lack of enthusiasm among certain culture groups regarding the use of modern technology and their reluctance to venturing into new enterprises has depressing impacts on the development impetus among some countries. As a result they remain at the low level of development. **India is a classic case** of the <u>**paradox of development and disparity**</u>.

There are certain regions which show high levels of human development while there are others that occupy the last position in the scale of development. India is a classical example in this respect.

Following conclusion can bc arrived at:

☐ Smaller states and union territories have recorded higher levels of human development than the larger states. This is indicative of the fact that in a largely state-sponsored and development-oriented economy like India, the large size as well as population of the administrative unit prove to be a deterrent as far as human development is concerned.

☐ States and union territories that have experienced development of basic infrastructure in the field of education and health facilities through the activities of voluntary organisations, non-governmental organisation and Missionary etc. have recorded higher levels of human development.

☐ Economic development is considered to be the basic requirement for better human development. But the experiences of different states of India indicate that in order to attain higher levels of human development mere economic development is not sufficient. States that show remarkable performance in the field of industrial and agricultural development have failed to register significant achievements in the field of human development.

☐ Certain communities may be laggard in terms of showing economic development and consequently form the geographical as well as the economic periphery of the country but they are very much part of the core as far as human development is concerned.

☐ There is a long way to go before India can match with other south Asian counties in terms of human development.

☐ To improve its current low position among the community of nations India will have to concentrate on development in the major states like UP, Bihar, Madhya Pradesh, Rajasthan, Assam and Andhra Pradesh, etc.

☐ For the larger state the Kerala model of development could be improvised to the state specific requirements.

9.3: IGNOU Past 6 Attempts Question - Solved

June 2019: Explain, how regional imbalances are a challenge to existing social order.   Answer by India Ebook: See Marked Concept

June 2019: Development means different things to different people. Comment.   Answer by India Ebook: Same as Q.1

June 2020: The concept of development assumes different meanings to different people in varying contexts.' Explain.

Answer by India Ebook: Same as Q.1

Dec 2020: Write short note: (a) Development as Freedom

Dec 2020: Write short note: (b) Sustainable Development

Answer by India Ebook: See Marked Concepts

10. AGRARIAN TRANSFORMATION AND LAND REFORMS

Introduction
Land Reforms
- ➢ Zamindari Abolition
- ➢ Cooperative Societies
- ➢ Bhoodan Movement
- ➢ Green Revolution

Impact of Land Reforms: Agrarian Transformation
- ➢ The Kulaks
- ➢ The Small Farmers and Landless Labourers

10.1: One Shot Concepts

INTRODUCTION

India has witnessed enormous agrarian transformation in the post-independence period. This has occurred due to the policies introduced by the state, which included land reforms, community development programmes, Green Revolution and several welfare schemes. As a result of the agrarian transformation a set of new classes and have emerged in rural society, while old groups or classes have either disappeared or have got transformed. The agrarian transformation has affected politics in India to a significant extent.

LAND REFORMS

➢ Zamindari Abolition

The first attempt to bring about the agrarian transformation was by the implementation of land reforms by states in India. Immediately after independence zamindari abolition bills or land tenure legislations were introduced in a number of states as UP, Madhya Pradesh, Bihar, Madras and Assam. **Land reforms in India** may be divided in to two phases. The first phase of land reforms started almost immediately after independence. It focused on institutional reforms and lasted till the early sixties, aimed at abolition of the intermediaries like zamindars and jagirdars. It provided ownership of land to the tenants or the security of tenure to tenants, reduction in rents and conferment of ownership rights on tenants. Another feature of this phase of land reforms was ceilings on landholdings. Apart from achieving these goals, the land reforms of this phase also aimed at community development programmes and cooperatives. The origin of the second phase can be traced to the middle of late sixties. This phase marked the beginning of the Green Revolution in India. **Green Revolution** attempted to introduce technological changes in certain states of the country, where favourable conditions for such change existed. Some of these states were Punjab, Haryana, Uttar Pradesh and Tamil Nadu. It introduce **dHYV (High Yielding Varieties of Seeds)**, new technology like tractors and irrigation facilities, etc. The main focus of the second phase has been technological reforms. The land reforms i.e., zamindari abolition and Green Revolution have brought tremendous changes in the agrarian sector.

A major problem faced at the time of **Implementation Of Zamindari Abolition Act** was the absence of adequate land records. By the year 1956 the intermediaries (zamindars and jagirdars) were abolished through a peaceful democratic method without use of coercive method. Because mostly the zamindars had sided with the British during the freedom struggle so they were an isolated class.

The zamindari abolition Acts in different parts of the country **suffered from many weaknesses**. In UP the zamindars were permitted to retain land under their personal cultivation. Personal cultivation was so loosely defined that it included even those who only supervised land personally or even through a relative or provided only capital or credit.

Only half of the land at the time of Independence was under zamindari system but the practice of tenancy existed even in the other half of the area, which were under the ryotwari system. Another important component of land reform–tenancy reform was also implemented not without hurdles. The legislations aiming at tenancy reforms passed by legislatures of different states and the methods of their implementation differed immensely because of different political and economic situation prevalent in different parts of the country.

> ➤ **Cooperative Societies**

Another important component of the first phase of land reforms was to encourage setting up of the cooperative societies in agriculture. It could be termed as cooperativisation of agriculture. Many of the top leaders of the Congress Party including **Nehru and Gandhi** along with the leaders of the **Socialist** and the **Communist Parties** were convinced about the benefit of cooperativisation. They shared this view that it would lead to major improvement in agriculture and which would also be beneficial to the poor. Cooperativisation constituted an important component of the fist phase of land reforms. But the goal of cooprativisation was also faced with the problem. Like in the case of land reforms there existed no consensus in favour of it among the peasantry.

The first five year plan recommended that small and medium farmers should be encouraged to group themselves in to cooperative farming societies. Another recommendation of the same plan was also that if majority of the occupancy tenants and landowners owing at least half of the land in a village wanted to enter into cooperative arrangement of the village land, their decision should be binding on other residents of the village also. The second five year plan declared that its objective was to provide sound foundations for the development of cooperative farming so that substantial portion of land could be cultivated on the lines of cooperative within a period of ten years.

In the field of cooperativisation China was the model because it had achieved dramatic results in agricultural production and extension of infrastructure through cooperativisation. In the middle of 1956 two Indian delegations consisting of the leaders of the cooperative movement, members of parliament bureaucrats with experience in the field of cooperatives and technical experts were sent to China to gain from their experience. The Nagpur Resolution of the Congress Party in 1959 underlined the twin needs of village panchayats and village cooperatives. This resolution also emphasised that these institutions should have enough powers and functions to discharge the functions allotted to them satisfactorily. This resolution aimed at achieving the goals of joint cooperative farming within and period of three years.

➢ **Bhoodan Movement**   June 2019

Bhoodan {land-gift} Movement launched in **April 1951** by **Acharya Vinoba Bhave**. The purpose of this movement was to appeal to the landowning classes to donate their surplus land to the poor. But the method adopted for this purpose by the movement was completely different from the one used in the abolition of Zamindari. Inspired by Gandhian technique the Sarvodya Samaj of Vinoba Bhave used the ideal of non-violent method of social transformation in to Bhoodan movement. The Vinoba Bhave and his band of followers traveled through villages on foot requesting the large landowners to donate one sixth of their land as bhoodan for distribution among the landless. Although the movement claimed to be independent, yet it enjoyed the support of the Congress Party. The All India Congress Committee had urged the Congressmen to support the movement.

Vinoba Bhave's experiment of **Bhoodan** started in 1951 Pochampali village in the Telangana region of Andhra. The choice of Telangna was significant because that area still felt reverberation of the armed peasant revolt led by the Communist Party of India. After its considerable success in Andhra the movement shifted to the northern part of the country.

In **1955 Vinoba Bhave's** experiment took another form, the form of **gram-dan (village-gift)**. The idea had its origin in Gandhian belief that all the land belonged to God. This movement was launched from a village in Orissa. In gram dan villages the movement declared that all the land was owned collectively or equally. The movement was very successful in Orissa. Later on it was launched in Maharashtra, Kerala and Andhra Pradesh.

> ➤ **Green Revolution**

The **Green Revolution** has been the main plank of the **second phase** of the land reforms. After independence in the rural sector the main focus was on institutional reforms in agriculture. By the late fifties and early sixties benefits from land reforms was reaching its limit. Around this time Nehru realised the need of technological solutions. The New Agricultural Strategy of picking up select areas with certain natural advantages for intensive development with package programme. The Intensive Agricultural District Programme was launched in the third five year plan. This programme picked up one district from each of the fifteen states on an experimental basis. In spite of these traces of the New Agricultural strategy the big push to it came only in the middle of the sixties. India was faced with chronic food shortage. The country had to resort to import of food grain from America under an agreement called PL480. In Bihar and UP there existed a famine like situation. In this kind of background some critical breakthrough in agricultural science showing promises of higher growth and possible solution of the food shortage launched India on the path of Green Revolution. The New Agricultural Strategy received wholehearted support from Prime Minister Lal Bahadur Shastri, Food Minister C. Subramaniam and Indira Gandhi who succeeded Shastri after his sudden death as Prime Minister.

The areas with **assured irrigation and other natural and institutional advantages** were provided with critical inputs like High Yielding Variety (HYV) seeds, chemical fertilizers and pesticides. Farmers in these areas were also given agricultural machinery like tractors, pumps–sets and tube–wells at convenient terms. They could avail the facility of soil testing agricultural credits and guidance from agricultural universities. Apart from providing these facilities to the farmers the government also set up an Agricultural Prices Commission in 1965. The purpose of this commission was to promise sustained remunerative price to the farmers. In this way the package of public investment, institutional credit, remunerative prices and easy availability of technological help made agriculture a profitable proposition. This New Agricultural Strategy or the Green Revolution led to phenomenal growth in agricultural production. Between 1968 to 1971 food grain production rose by 35 per cent. Very soon India buried its begging bowl image and by the 1980s emerged as a country not only with buffer food stock but also as a food supplier.

IMPACT OF LAND REFORMS: AGRARIAN TRANSFORMATION — Book Q.1

> ### The Kulaks — Book Q.3

Land reforms, especially the Zamindari abolition and Green Revolution had enormous impact on the agrarian transformation. On the one hand these accelerated the agriculture growth; on the other, entire pattern of the relations in agriculture underwent transformation. The latter was reflected in the rise of a class of economically and politically powerful groups in several parts of India. They came to be popularly known as Kulaks or rich farmers. L.H. Rudolph and Sussan Rudolph categoried them as "bullock capitalists". These groups emerged to control the political affairs in several states, and from the 1990s they have become influential in the national politic as well. In terms of the caste composition, they belonged to the intermediary castes like Jats, Yadavs, Lodhs, Gujars, Kurmie, etc., in Uttar Pradesh, Haryana, Punjab and Rajasthan; Marathas in Maharastra; Lingayats and Vokaliggas in Karnataka; and Reddies and Kammas in Andhra Pradesh. They have been identified as the OBCs in the states inhabited by them. Having become the owners of land following the Zamindari abolition, they benefited from the modern technologies and inputs through Green Revolution. The land reforms made them the most powerful groups in the agrarian society in many regions of the country. The emergence also resulted in the decline of the erstwhile dominant groups. The developments, however, did not benefit the socially and economically vulnerable groups – dalits and the lower backward classes. The welfare measures like the poverty alleviation programmes, etc. have been mainly the populist measures.

Besides, these have been hampered by large scale corruption. Nevertheless, due to the spread of education, awareness and impart of the ideas of **Dr. B.R. Ambedkar** and mass media, there has been the assertion of dalits in certain including the rural areas states like Uttar Pradesh. The emergence of the Bahujan Samaj Party is an indication of this. Kulaks or rich farmers have made their presence felt through their political parties and nonpolitical organisations. The **first example** of such attempt was foundation of the **Bharatiya Kranti Dal** (BKD) by Charan Singh. In the late 1970s and 1980s – the organisation like the Bharatiya Kisan Union (BKU) in North India, Shetkari Sangathan in Maharastra and Karnataka Ryat Sangha in Karnataka played important role in articulating the interests of Kulaks.

> ➢ **The Small Farmers and Landless Labourers**

In the 1960s and 1970s large part of the country witnessed the emergence of the movement of the small farmers and landless labour. This movement started from Naxalbari in West Bengal and very soon spread to different parts of country like Andhra Pradesh, Bihar and Orissa till the end of the 60s. In 1970 a land grab movement of the landless led by the Socialist Party and the Communist Party of India was witnessed in Gujarat, Punjab, Rajasthan, Tamil Nadu, Andhra Pradesh and Bihar.

Although these movements could not achieve much yet they succeeded in attracting the attention of the countrymen towards agrarian question. The Left front government introduced land reforms in West Bengal during its tenure. This ensured the security to the tenants and land to the tiller. In 1970 while addressing Chief Ministers conference on land reforms the Prime Minister Indira Gandhi held that the cause of discontent in the countryside was the failure of the land reforms to meet the expectation of the people in the countryside. Reduction in ceiling limits was the main proposal discussed in this conference. Most of the Chief Ministers rejected this proposal. Then this matter was referred to the Central Land Reforms Committee. This committee made quite a few recommendations in 1971. The 1972 Chief Ministers' conference approved some national guidelines for reforms in India. The national guidelines made a departure from the history of ceiling legislation in India. It reduced the ceiling limits on all categories of lands. Family, not individual was taken as unit for the purpose of ceiling. Preference was to be given to landless labourers, particularly belonging to scheduled castes and scheduled tribes in distribution of surplus lands. The compensation this time was much below the market price. The landowners again went to court and indulged in other deceitful methods to undermine the ceiling laws. Nevertheless, in the 1970s the ceiling legislation moderately succeeded in its objective of collecting and distributing surplus land. Another good thing was that the major-beneficiaries of the ceiling laws this time were the scheduled castes and scheduled tribes.

10.2: IGNOU Book Exercise - Solved

1) Explain the relationships between land reforms and agrarian transformation.

Answer by India Ebook: Read the 1 Shot Concept Above.

2) What were the limitations of land reforms?

Answer by India Ebook: Land tenure reforms are the only ones covered by the term "land reforms." The Latin word "teneo," from which the term "tenure" is derived, means "to hold." Thus, the term "land tenure" is used to describe the circumstances surrounding the ownership of land. Since they aim to end exploitative relationships marked by stark inequalities between wealthy landowners and destitute peasants without security of tenure, land reforms are seen as a tool for social justice.

By placing limits on the extent of holdings that a family can acquire, it takes a step against the accumulation of landholdings in the hands of a small number of absentee/non-cultivating proprietors. Although redistribution of land is the common understanding of land reforms, their scope is far broader.

The main advantage of such land reforms is that they increase the country's agricultural output. Without a substantial input of governmental funding, this is accomplished. India already struggled to provide for its own food needs. These land modifications provide a cost-free way to increase the production of grains and other agricultural goods on farms. The farmer will also sell the extra produce to the market once he has enough to eat to help the economy.

The government and farmers' relationships improved as a result of these land reforms. Under British rule, these farmers were badly exploited, which resulted in their disenfranchisement. These adjustments made it possible for farmers and the government to connect. Together, they strengthened the agriculture sector of our economy.

Sharecropping, landlordism, and other institutions survived in many places despite the end of the zamindari.

- Only the top layer of landlords was removed from the multi-layered agricultural structure.
- It led to widespread evictions.
- There are several social, economic, administrative, and legal problems as a result of mass eviction.

3) Write a note on the role of Kulaks in politics.

Answer by India Ebook: Read the 1 Shot Concept Above.

10.3: IGNOU Past 6 Attempts Question – Solved

June 2019: Write short note: (b) Bhoodan Movement

Answer by India Ebook: Refer Concepts Above.

June 2020: Briefly describe the policies introduced by the state that have contributed to agrarian transformation in India.

Answer: Same as Q.1 Above

Dec 2020: Examine the State policies that have contributed to agrarian transformation in India.

June 2021: Write short note: (a) Cooperative movement in India

June 2021: Write short note: (b) Ceiling on land holdings

Answer above 3: Refer Concepts Above.

11. INDUSTRY AND LABOUR

Introduction

Industry

- ➢ National Industrial Policy
- ➢ States in the National Industrial Policy
- ➢ States and Economic Reforms
- ➢ States and Industries

Labour

- ➢ Labour and States
- ➢ Industrial Disputes
- ➢ Labour and Social Security
- ➢ Labur and Privatisation

11.1: One Shot Concepts

INTRODUCTION

The Indian federation the states in India enjoy considerable political autonomy to pursue their own policies in the areas of industrial relations. Myron Weiner says that distribution of power between center and states is the cornerstone of Indian democratic system. State governments manage State public sector enterprise and play an important role in shaping industrial relations and labour policies. The state governments also have a voice in the national government. The Chief Ministers of states are members of National Development Council, which plays an important role in shaping economic and social policies of the country. Although state governments are not officially represented in the union cabinet, Prime Ministers so far have taken care to give every state its share of representatives. The central government is dependent on the state governments for carrying out its important decisions. They function as regulatory authority over industrial enterprises, small business.

INDUSTRY

➢ National Industrial Policy

At the time of independence India had inherited a backward economy. What was worse was that a few states were industrialised and richer, while others subsisted mainly on agriculture and were poor states. The port towns of Bombay, Calcutta and Madras had emerged as centers of industrial activities. This created job opportunities. Educational institutions and other facilities also came up in these centers. These developments led to emergence of some consumer industries, which in turn led to emergence of merchant capitalist class with surplus to invest in industry.

These factors gave these areas a head start. The country had to aim at having rapid development but the growth was not to be achieved at the cost of justice. As envisaged in the Directive Principles of State Policy it had to ensure adequate means of livelihood to all its citizens and also that operation of economic system should not result in concentration of wealth in the hands of few. Self-reliant growth was another goal. It also aimed at balanced development of the country.

The **Industrial Policy Resolution of 1956** provided for what came to be known as mixed economy. Public and private sectors were to exist side by side. Even foreign firms were allowed to operate. The economy had to function within governmental planning and control. Public monopoly had to be established over manufacturing of arms and ammunition, atomic energy and railway. The government reserved the right to start new enterprise in coal, iron steel and other minerals, ship building, manufacture of aircrafts and telephone and telegraph equipments.

In **1955** at its **Avadi session** the **Indian National Congress** declared the establishment of socialistic pattern of society as its goal. In spite of this commitment by the Congress Party the Industrial Policy Resolution of 1956 did not mention any thing about nationalisation. Actually this resolution reaffirmed India's commitment to mixed economy. In the projected model public and private sectors were not only to coexist they also had to complement each other. Private sectors were to be encouraged and given all possible freedom within the objectives of planning. An important part of the strategy was rapid development of heavy and capital goods industry under public sector. The shift in favour of heavy industry was to be combined with promotion of labour intensive small and cottage industries producing consumer goods. This aimed at tackling the problems of unemployment.

➢ States in the National Industrial Policy

It is obvious that the path of development chosen by India after Independence assigned very important role to state not only at national level but also at the regional level. State governments also had to play important role in establishment of public sectors and controlling private sectors.

Almost all the states set up State Electricity Boards, State Transport Corporations, State Financial Corporations and State Tourism Corporation. Many states set up cooperatives for farmers. Some states set up Textile Corporation and Khadhi Boards. At the instance of Planning Commission the institute of Public Enterprise had compiled some information regarding State Level Public Enterprises. According to it information, on March 31, 1986, there were 636 State Level Public Sector Enterprises functioning in 24 States with investment to the tune of Rs. 10,000 crores. If investment in State Electricity Boards and State Transport Corporation is added, the total investment stood at 25,000 crore. In 1977 this figure stood at 950 crore. In this way it is obvious that State Level Public Sector witnessed a growth of 20 percent between 1977-86. On March 31, 2000 the total investment in State Level Public Sector Units was to the tune of 1,62,063 crores. Gujrat, Maharashtra, Karnatka, Uttar Pradesh, West Bengal and Punjab accounted for 63.6% of the total investment in all the State Level Public Sector Units.

➢ States and Economic Reforms

Faced with a situation of loss making public sector units and inelastic source of revenue the states have no choice but to reform. In spite of this the state governments do not exhibit uniform attitude towards reforms. Many state governments are still following the pre-reform mindset.

Some of the states have realised the need of reforms. Orissa government reformed its State Electricity Boards and Gujarat, Maharashtra, Tamil Nadu, Andhra Pradesh and Karnatka sought to create investment friendly climate. On the basis of per capita income, literacy state, domestic product states have been classified as forward and backward states. The list of forward states include Punjab, Maharashtra, Haryana, Gujarat, West Bengal, Karnatka, Kerala, Tamil Nadu and Andhra Pradesh . The list of backward states includes Madhya Pradesh, Assam, Uttar Pradesh,

Rajasthan, Orissa and Bihar. N.J. Kurian indicated that in the post-reform period two thirds of investment proposals were concentrated in the forward regions. A clear cut bias in favuor of forward states can be seen even in matters of financial assistance distributed by national and state financial institutions like IDBI, IFCI, ICICI, UTI and ISDBI. The forward states cornered 67.3% of financial assistance distributed by these institutions till March 1997. Even within the category of forward states Maharashtra, Gujarat, Tamil Nadu and Andhra Pradesh appropriated 51% of the total assistance. This is obvious that the reform process has favoured the forward states as they have succeeded in attracting the lions share of investment proposals and financial assistance. This would further accelerate the growth process in the forward states while the backward states face the prospect of growth retardation.

➢ **States and Industries**   Book Q.2

At the time of independence a national capitalist class had come into existence. The Marwari enterprise had acquired a base in such far off places as Calcutta, Madras, Hyderabad and Kanpur. Gujarati enterprise was well settled in Bombay, although Parsi enterprise was localised in western India. By the 1960s, after almost two decades of industrial development, most private investment was controlled either by multinational companies or by the Marwari, Gujarati and Parsi enterprise which had made best use of the opportunities that came along. Obviously there was concentration of economic power in the hands of a handful of business houses that was not in consonance with the stated goals in the **Directive Principles** of State Policy.

The regional capitalists are first generation in business. Generally their business is confined to their state of domicile. This class has sprung from different background. Some of them come from agricultural families. Others have there capital coming from trade and commerce. Many of them come from the families of professionals gainfully employed in India or abroad. They have entered diverse type of industries ranging from textiles, cement, sugar, chemicals, fertilizers, pharmaceuticals, electronics, steel and engineering goods. While in1950s and 1960s in states like Andhra Pradesh, Gujarat, Maharashtra and Punjab large scale manufacturing units were set up either in public sector or by national big business houses like Birla, Thapar, Shriram etc. The 1980s onwards a big share of investment opportunity has been grabbed by regional capitalists. They have entered industries like cement, sugar, pharmaceuticals and electronics in a big way. The national big business houses had supported and funded the Congress Party hence they were in a position to influence the policy of the Congress Party. The national big houses kept doing so for four years after the independence. The regional capitalists faced discrimination at the hands of Congress ruled central governments. This was also true about national financial institutions like Industrial Development Bank of India and Industrial Finance Corporation of India. Many of the states like Gujarat, Maharashtra, Punjab, Andhra Pradesh, Karnatka and Tamil Nadu have pretty active capital market. A very large number of capital issues are subscribed here. The emergence of stock exchanges in Andhra Pradesh, Karnatka, Kerala, Tamil Nadu,

Uttar Pradesh, West Bengal and Delhi indicate towards a vibrant capital market in these states. The success of regional capitalist class has become possible because of the supportive role played by the state governments and also the state level leaders. The bias of a highly centralised Congress Party of the Indera-Rajeev era in favour of national business class also pushed the entrepreneurs in states towards regional political parties for support. With the decline of the dominance of the Congress Party a phase of coalition has emerged.

LABOUR

➢ Labour and States

State level public sectors together are much bigger employer than public sectors under the central government. Nearly 7.3 million workers are employed by state governments. While the number of people employed under central government is 3.4 million. Employment in central government has grown only marginally while state governments have added another million. As the State governments also manage many public sectors at the state level they play important role in shaping both industrial relation and labour policies. State governments play an important role in settling industrial disputes and running social security schemes for workers. In agricultural sector also state governments play major role in fixation and implementation of Minimum Wages. In cases of private sector units deciding to close down or retrench the labour, permission of the concerned state government is to be taken in advance. Public sectors at the state level have been vehicles for creating jobs.

According to a 1981 census data agricultural labour constituted 26.3 per cent of the total labour force. According to Second Labour Enquiry published in 1960 more than 85 per cent of the rural workers are casual, serving any farmer ready to engage them. Nearly 15 per cent of agricultural labourers are attached to specific landlords. More than half of workers do not possess any land and even rest of them own only very little of land. Another fact about them is that they predominantly belong to scheduled caste scheduled tribe and other backward classes. In 1948 Minimum Wages Act was passed. This Act asked every State government to fix minimum wages for agricultural labour within three years. Only in a few states of India agricultural labour get the minimum wages notified by the government.

A notification of the central government directed the state governments in 1998 not to fix the minimum wages in the unorganised sector below Rs 40. Only Haryana, Punjab, Mizoram, Manipur, Rajasthan, Uttar Pradesh adhere to this rate.In most states minimum wages were fixed between 1995-96. The range of variation in minimum wages between the states is very large. In Haryana where it is highest it ranges between Rs. 63.12 – Rs. 64.12 in Punjab between Rs. 58.07 – Rs. 60.62. In Andhra Pradesh it is Rs. 16 – Rs. 42.40 and in Bihar it is between Rs. 27.30 – Rs. 39.70.

> ### ➢ **Industrial Disputes**

Industrial disputes result in stoppage of production. These disputes affect national income. They also cause inconvenience to consumers. In the case of industrial labour state governments together with central government play an important role in settling conflicts between capitalists and labour.

In 1947 the government of India passed the Industrial Disputes Act. This Act outlined the machinery for prevention and settlement of disputes. This act was amended in 1956. This amended Act provided for machinery for settlement of disputes. State governments have set up labour courts to go into disputed orders of employers. These courts also go into dismissals and suspensions of employees. They are also empowered to go in to legality or otherwise of strikes and lockouts. The State governments have power to appoint one or more tribunals. These tribunals adjudicate disputes relating to wages, bonus, profit, etc. The state tribunals are headed by a person of the rank of a High Court Judge. In 1967 National Arbitration Promotion Board was set up the government. Its objective was to promote voluntary arbitration to settle industrial disputes. The Board includes representatives of employers and workers and Central and State Governments.

> **Labour and Social Security**

In the Industrial sector workers have to face periodic unemployment due to what is known as cyclical fluctuation in business, sickness, industrial accidents and old age. While the capitalists have all the resources to face the uncertainies of business the workers do not have resources to fall back upon when faced with unemployment, old age, sickness or accidents. States have an obligation towards them. With this objective in view Employee's State Insurance Act was passed in 1948. This Act provides for cash benefit during sickness, maternity and employment injury. Pension on the death of a worker and payment of funeral expenses in the event of death of an insured person. This Act also provides for medical care and treatment. The Act covers wage earners, low paid clerical and administrative staff whose salary is below Rs 6500. This Act created an autonomous body named Employees State Insurance Corporation with the responsibility of administering the scheme. The governing body of the Corporation has 40 persons representing both Union and State governments, the Parliament, employers' and employees' organisations and medical professionals. The Act also created a Employees' State Insurance Fund. The employers contribution which was earlier fixed at 4 per cent has been raised to 4.75 per cent. The employees' contribution has gone up from 1.5 per cent to 1.75 per cent of wage. Besides, the contribution of employers' and employees' the scheme is dependent on grants from central and state governments. On medical care the state government shares to the extent of 12.5 per cent. In 1961 Maternity Benefit Act was passed. This Act intended to provide uniform standards for maternity protection. The Act applies to all factories, mines and plantations not covered by Emloyees' State Insurance Act. The Act provides for maternity benefit at rate of average daily wages for a total period of 12 weeks.

> ### **Labour and Privatisation** Book Q.3

The organised sector [Emloyment in public sectors and private sectors employing more than ten persons] emloys 8.34 per cent of the labour force. The organised sector is suffering from a near jobless growth. Between 1993-94 to 1999-2000 the public sector made a very small contribution to creation of jobs. As part of the New Economic Policy the policy of downsising has started. This means reducing overheads for cost reduction. In plain terms downsizing means loss of jobs. Privatisation also is seen as a threat to jobs. Closure of sick industries also makes the employees jobless.

Retrenchment Voluntry Retirement Schemes and Casualisation seems to characterise the condition of labour in the post reform phase. Industrial Disputes Act 1947 lays reasonable restrictions on employers intending to undertake retrenchment or closure. In such cases due notice will have to be given to the union and the union and the management will devise ways and means to protect employment of the workers. On the grounds of economic rationality these provisions are sought to be changed. In the developed countries downsising is less painful because of fully developed sobcial security system. That is not the case with developing countries like ours. Due to this fear labour in organised sector is opposed to privatisation. Ashutosh Varshney is of the view that privatisation should be decoupled from large scale retrenchment only then it will be easier to launch bigger privatisation programmes. Tata Steel bought OMC Alloys in Orissa in 1991 but without firing the workers its productivity went up. Even Delhi Vidut Board has been sold but the workers have not faced retrenchment.

In this kind of situation only unorganised sector seems to have potential for future employment because this sector employs 92 per cent of the labour force. The unorganised sector of the economy includes both small business and the self-employed. The main employment generating activity in the unorganised sectors are agriculture and allied activities, trade, restaurants and hotels and tourism. It also includes social sectors like education and health. Transport and construction are also part of it. Even information - technology is part of the unorganised sector. The unorganised sector has 3.8 times more employment elasticity than the organised sector. The agricultural sector can become labour absorbing if focus is given on areas like horticulture, floriculture, agro-forestry minor irrigation and watershed development. Another high potential employment generating area in unorganised sector are trade, restaurants and tourism and information technology. These areas are witnessing a high growth of above 9 per cent.

11.2: IGNOU Book Exercise – Solved

1) Identify the features of industrial policy as envisaged in the Avadi session of the Indian National Congress.

Answer by India Ebook: The Industrial Policy Resolution of 1956 provided for what came to be known as mixed economy. Public and private sectors were to exist side by side. Even foreign firms were allowed to operate. The economy had to function within governmental planning and control. Public monopoly had to be established over manufacturing of arms and ammunition, atomic energy and railway. The government reserved the right to start new enterprise in coal, iron steel and other minerals, ship building, manufacture of aircrafts and telephone and telegraph equipments.In **1955** at its **Avadi session** the **Indian National Congress** declared the establishment of socialistic pattern of society as its goal. In spite of this commitment by the Congress Party the Industrial Policy Resolution of 1956 did not mention any thing about nationalisation. Actually this resolution reaffirmed India's commitment to mixed economy. In the projected model public and private sectors were not only to coexist they also had to complement each other. Private sectors were to be encouraged and given all possible freedom within the objectives of planning. An important part of the strategy was rapid development of heavy and capital goods industry under public sector. The shift in favour of heavy industry was to be combined with promotion of labour intensive small and cottage industries producing consumer goods. This aimed at tackling the problems of unemployment.

2) What are the pattern of industrialisation in Indian States?

Answer by India Ebook: Read the 1 Shot Concept Above.

3) Discuss the impact of privitisation on working class.

Answer by India Ebook: Read the 1 Shot Concept Above.

11.3: IGNOU Past 6 Attempts Question – Solved

June 2021: Examine the role of states in industrialisation in the post-reform period.

Answer by India Ebook: Refer Concept: States and Economic Reforms

12. GLOBALISATION AND LIBERALISATION: IMPLICATIONS FOR STATE POLITICS

Introduction

Paradigm of Economic Development

Economic Reforms and Foreign Direct Investment

Economic Liberalisation: Divergent Views

Globalisation and its Impact on State Politics

12.1: One Shot Concepts

INTRODUCTION

In 1991 the government of India launched the New Economic Policy that ushered in the phase of liberalisation and globalisation in India. Liberalisation and globalisation are inter-related concepts. Liberalisation has come to mean a policy of industrial delicensing, deregulation and disinvestments and privatisation of the public sector; globalisation means opening the economy for foreign investment, removing restrictions to international trade and becoming part of the World Trade Organisation.

The policy of liberalisation and globalisation has become synonymous with policy of economic reforms. Although the general practice is to locate the beginning of the economic reforms from 1991, yet traces of economic reforms can be seen in the economic policies followed by Indira Gandhi's government since 1980.The economic policies followed by the Rajeev Gandhi's government can be seen as a precursor to the economic policies unfolding after 1991.

The present Prime Minister Dr. Manmohan Singh and economists like Jagdish Bhagwati have been among the early supporters of economic reforms. While the policy of globalisation and liberalisation is defended in the name of faster economic growth, its critics see it as or anti-poor policy. Some even perceive it as a surrender to the international capital. More than two decades have passed since the country was launched on the path of economic reforms.

The policy of globalisation and liberalisation has affected the lives of our country men in a big way. Their implications on State Politics have been far reaching. The policy of liberalisation and globalisation has led to the emergence of the regional capitalist class. A symbiotic relationship seems to have developed between the regional capitalists and the regional political parties. Many of the state governments have been vying with each other in attracting foreign capital. The new developments call for a fresh understanding of the centre state relations. The inter-state relations have also assumed significance in the context of New Economic Policy.

PARADIGM OF ECONOMIC DEVELOPMENT

Before the introduction of the New Economic Policy in1991 by the Congress government led - by P.V. Narasimha Rao, the Indian Economy was control –ridden, inward looking and one of the insulated economies among the Third World countries. In 1991 the country was faced with an unprecedented economic crisis with the balance of payment situation reaching or critical point. The foreign exchange reserve of the country was barely enough to pay for the imports of two months. The country had no option but to approach the World Bank and the IMF for loans to tide over its economic crisis. To procure these loans, the country had to agree to a package of Stabilisation and Structural Adjustment Programme. This package gave the needed boost to the liberalisation process of the Indian economy. To break through the traditional mindset opposing economic reforms, the government used the crisis in the economy to embark on the path of comprehensive economic reforms.

The package of reforms that ensued in 1991 involved the **devaluation of the rupee** by twenty per cent. This was aimed at linking the rupee realistically to the market. Provisions for freer access to imports were made. The license control system was dismantled with the abolition of the Monopolistic and Restrictive Trade Practices which were taking place in public sectors as well with a shift towards gradual privatisation. These reforms also included the reforms in the capital market and the financial sector. The attitude on multinational companies and foreign investment witnessed a complete turn around. Restrictions gave way to reception.

ECONOMIC REFORMS AND FOREIGN DIRECT INVESTMENT

India had set out on the path of economic recovery by following the path of **economic reforms**. The Gross Domestic Product (GDP) that had fallen to a paltry 0.8 per cent in the year 1991-92, had gone up to 6.2 per cent by 1993-94. During the Eighth Five year Plan period, the economy recorded the growth rate of around seven per cent. This rate of growth was pretty close to that of high performance economies of East Asia. This remarkable feat was achieved in spite of the pangs of crisis and structural adjustment. Other economic indices like Gross Domestic Saving had also witnessed an upward swing. The growth rate of Industrial production registered an increase from a meager 1% in 1991-92 to 6% in 1993-94.

Exports that had registered a decline of 1.5% in 1991 (term of dollar) started showing signs of a steady growth. Between 1993-96, it registered a growth rate of around 20%. It was in tune with the objective of self-reliant growth. A considerably larger proportion of imports were now paid for by exports. The ratio of export earnings to import payments raised from an average of 60 per cent in the eighties to nearly 90% by the mid 1990s. The foreign exchange reserves in 1991 which were barely enough to pay for the imports of two weeks had now become enough to pay for the imports of seven months by the end of January 1999.

The opening up of the economy encouraged foreign investment to a great deal. Between 1991 to 1996, the foreign direct investment grew at the rate of 100% per year. From $129 million in 1991-92, it touched the figure of $2.1 billion in 1995-96. It was a commendable achievement but on this score, the country still lagged behind the East Asian countries. For example, China has been receiving foreign direct investment to the tune of $30 billion annually. An important development was the gradual erosion of hostility against foreign capital.

After 1995-96, when the growth rate reached a peak of 12.8%, there has been a decline to 5.5 and 6.6 in the next two years. This slowing down of the economy is partly seen as an impact of the recession in Japan, South Korea, Indonesia, Thailand and other nations. Around this time these economies were recording negative growth and even the world trade had slowed down in 1998. It was also blamed that India could not address itself to structural process inhibiting growth.

There has not been much of resistance from the rich farmers. India joined the World Trade Organisation when the Government of India signed the

Uruguay Round of the General Agreement on Tariffs and Trade (GATT) at Maracas in 1994. As per the conditions of the GATT, the developing countries including India are under an obligation to introduce subsidies where they were asked to keep subsidies to the farmers up to 10 per cent of their value output. India, with other countries of the Third World, has accused the WTO of following discriminatory practices. The developed countries continue to give subsidies while they pressurise the developing countries to cut subsidies. As is obvious, cutting subsidies would hurt the interests of the farmers. The response of the rich farmers towards the New Economic Policy or India becoming part of the WTO has not been undifferentiated.

ECONOMIC LIBERALISATION: DIVERGENT VIEWS

Book Q.2

One of the major criticisms of the policy of economic reforms has been on the ground that the reforms have been anti-poor. It is argued that these reforms have an inbuilt bias in favour of the upper and middle classes and hurt the interests of the underprivileged in material sense. It is argued that these reforms would further aggravate economic inequality, and this is in conflict with the constitutional goal of creating a just society. Economic equality is an essential component of this conception of a just society. One of the basic objectives of the policy makers since inception of planning has been to achieve growth with justice. The supporters of the reformist agenda refuse to accept the view that economic reforms would aggravate economic inequality. On the contrary they argue that a rapid economic growth, in fact, is associated with a fall in poverty levels.

Another criticism of the liberalisation and globalisation process has been that it would lead to job loss. Privatisation of the public sector has faced resistance from organised labour. Workers have been pushed out under what has come to be known as voluntary retirement scheme. Contract and casual labour have started substituting regular employees. A number of unviable units have been closed through various subterfuges. Under the policy of privatisation several important public sector units in the country have been sold to the private companies.

Some critics have also started arguing that the economic reforms have led to a period of jobless growth. Globalisation and liberalisation are creating job opportunities for the highly trained manpower like the graduates from IITs and Indian Institute of Management; similarly the call centres give jobs to those having a good command over English. People coming from upper middle class and urban background have a clear advantage in getting such jobs with astronomical salary. The policy of reservation in government jobs has been based on the idea of social justice, because without reservation, candidates from disadvantaged background were unable to get jobs.

Some economists are of the view that policies like trade liberalisation gives multinational corporations an opportunity to capture the Third World market at the expense of the local producers. Opening up opportunities for foreign investment in the third world countries offers to the MNCs an opportunity to earn huge profit. The United Progressive Alliance government that came to power in 2004 pledged itself to carry on with the policy of reforms decided to give reforms with a human face. The Common Minimum Programme of the UPA gave the needed emphasis on the needs of farmers and poor people because the reforms so far are said to have a bias in favour of urban and the rich sections of the Indian society.

GLOBALISATION AND ITS IMPACT ON STATE POLITICS

Book Q.3 & Q.4

The policy of globalisation and liberalisation has, in a way, created a situation in which the state governments have emerged as the real focus of power and decision - making. State governments have been engaged in an unbridled competition to attract foreign capital. The foreign investors have to deal with the state governments for establishing their projects. The decade of 1990s has also been described as political refederalisation of India without changing the constitution.

A centralised political system has been an essential part of the Indian economic planning in which the state governments were led by the central government. Economic reforms demand an effective role from the state governments. The process of liberalisation and globalisation is throwing up new challenges to the Indian federalism and it appears to be restructuring power relations between the centre and the states. Some illustrations can substantiate these points in a better way. The old system of centre-State relations had evolved a system of centrally sponsored schemes implemented by state governments but funded by the central government. In the new trend the central government seems to be unburdening itself and passing on the responsibilities of economic development of states to state governments. In the new scenario state governments have emerged as important economic actors in place of the central governments. But the retreat of the central government from the management of the national economy is likely to aggravate inter–state or inter-regional disparities.

India, at the time of independence, had inherited all kinds of regional imbalances. From the beginning one of the major goals of planning in India has been balanced development. It seems that with the launch of the New Economic Policy the commitment to the balanced development of India came to an end. The 1990s has witnessed state governments struggling to fight their own battle. If a state can offer an attractive package to the foreign investor, that state is considered as forward looking, reformist and progressive.

Centralisation, under the license-permit raj, created a rift between those who could effectively lobby the central government, and others whose political and business influence was restricted to a state or a region within that state. Unlike the merchant capitalist and largely metropolitan origins of the national big business groups, the new generation of regional business group have agrarian origin and rural roots. The regional business looked at licensing system of the national government as inequitable benefiting big business.

12.2: IGNOU Book Exercise - Solved

1) What are the factors that led India to follow the path of economic reforms?

Answer by India Ebook: India had set out on the path of economic recovery by following the path of **economic reforms**. The Gross Domestic Product (GDP) that had fallen to a paltry 0.8 per cent in the year 1991-92, had gone up to 6.2 per cent by 1993-94. During the Eighth Five year Plan period, the economy recorded the growth rate of around seven per cent. This rate of growth was pretty close to that of high performance economies of East Asia. This remarkable feat was achieved in spite of the pangs of crisis and structural adjustment. Other economic indices like Gross Domestic Saving had also witnessed an upward swing. The growth rate of Industrial production registered an increase from a meager 1% in 1991-92 to 6% in 1993-94.

Exports that had registered a decline of 1.5% in 1991 (term of dollar) started showing signs of a steady growth. Between 1993-96, it registered a growth rate of around 20%. It was in tune with the objective of self-reliant growth. A considerably larger proportion of imports were now paid for by exports. The ratio of export earnings to import payments raised from an average of 60 per cent in the eighties to nearly 90% by the mid 1990s. The foreign exchange reserves in 1991 which were barely enough to pay for the imports of two weeks had now become enough to pay for the imports of seven months by the end of January 1999.

There has not been much of resistance from the rich farmers. India joined the World Trade Organisation when the Government of India signed the **Uruguay Round** of the General Agreement on Tariffs and Trade (GATT) at Maracas in 1994. As per the conditions of the GATT, the developing countries including India are under an obligation to introduce subsidies where they were asked to keep subsidies to the farmers up to 10 per cent of their value output. India, with other countries of the Third World, has accused the WTO of following discriminatory practices.

2) Discuss the divergent views on India's policy of economic reforms.

Answer by India Ebook: Read the 1 Shot Concept Above.

3) What are the **implications** of **globalisation** on the state politics in India?

Answer by India Ebook: Read the 1 Shot Concept Above.

4) "The retreat of the central government from the management of the national economy will aggravate inter-state disparities". Substantiate this statement.

Answer by India Ebook: Read the 1 Shot Concept Above.

12.3: IGNOU Past 6 Attempts Question – Solved

Dec 2020: Critically examine the impact of globalisation on State politics in India.

Answer by India Ebook: Almost same as Q.3 above.

13. INTER-STATE DISPUTES: WATER AND TERRITORIAL BOUNDARIES

Introduction

Water Disputes

> ➢ Uneven Availability of Water
> ➢ River Basins
> ➢ Politics of Water Disputes

The Boundary Disputes

> ➢ A Colonial Legacy
> ➢ Territorial Issue in the Post-Colonial Period
> ➢ The Belgaun Dispute: An Example

13.1: One Shot Concepts

INTRODUCTION

The inter-state relations in India run along the lines of both conflict and cooperation. The apecifics of each case depend on the nature of constitutional provisions regarding these relations, attitudes of the institutions involved, concerned leaderships and political circumstances. There are disputes among Indian states over sharing of a natural resource like water and over boundaries. The disputes have resulted in violent clashes between states on several occasions. Their failure or success in handling the disputes is indicative of functioning of the Indian federalism.

WATER DISPUTES

Water is one of the most important requirements of human beings. It is used for multi-purposes – drinking, cleanliness, agriculture and industries. Its shortage or absence can lead to disputes in society. Its unequal distribution among states can disturb the federal relations. Water disputes arising from the need in agriculture for irrigation has had the most effective political expression im our country. Before discussing the cases of water disputes, it is relevant to discuss the unevenness of water availability and the river basin in India.

> ### ➢ Uneven Availability of Water

India is considered rich in terms of annual rainfall and total water resources available at the national level. However, the uneven distribution of the resource causes regional and temporal shortages. India's average annual rainfall, about 4000 billion cubic meters (BCM) is unevenly distributed, both spatially as well as temporally. The annual per capita utilisable resource availability varies from 18,417cubic meters in the Brahmaputra Valley to as low as 180 cubic meters in the Sabarmati Basin. Even in the Ganga Basin, the annual per capita availability of water varies from 740 cubic meters (cu m) in the Yamuna to 3,379 cum in the Gandak. Levels of precipitation vary from 100 mm annually in western Rajasthan to over 9,000 mm in the north-eastern state of Meghalaya. With 75 percent of the rainfall occurring over the four monsoon months and the other 1000 BCM spread over the remaining eight months, the Indian rivers carry 90% of the water between June and November. Thus, only 10% of the river flow is available during the other six month. India can, however, boast of a good network of rivers flowing through different parts and sustaining the economy.

> ### River Basins

The country's rivers have been classified as Himalayan, peninsular, coastal and inland-drainage basin rivers. Himalayan rivers are snow fed and maintain a high to medium rate of flow throughout the year. The heavy annual average rainfall levels in the Himalayan catchment areas further add to their rates of flow. During the monsoon months of June to September, the catchment areas are prone to flooding. The volume of the rain-fed peninsular rivers also increases. Coastal streams, especially in the west, are short and episodic. Rivers of the inland system, centered in western Rajasthan state, are few and frequently disappear in years of scant rainfall. The majority of the rivers flow through broad, shallow valleys and drain into the Bay of Bengal.

River basin as a unit of understanding the river flow through different states provides a scientific approach. The basin area is the extent of the area from where water may be expected in the river. It includes tributaries and even drains. Indian rivers have been divided into three categories depending on basin area. Major rivers are those rivers whose basin area is 20,000 square km. or more. The river basin areas in between 2,000 and 20,000 square kilometers are grouped as medium rivers and the rest are minor rivers. Major river basins are 13 in number and as a group they cover 80% of the population and 85 per cent of total river discharge.

Three **major rivers** i.e. the **Ganga**, the **Brahmaputra** and the **Indus** are snow-fed rivers, originating in the Himalayas. The **other ten rivers** originate either in Central India or in the peninsular regions. These rivers are Godavari, Krishna, Pennar, Mahanadi, Cauvery, Narmada, Tapi, Brahmani, Mahi and Sabarmati. The medium river basins are forty-five in number while the minor river basins are fifty five. Thus, the **113 river basins** ranging from major to medium to minor based on their basin areas transcend different political boundaries.

Harnessing the waters of the major rivers that flow through different states is therefore, an issue of great concern. Issues of flood control, drought prevention, hydroelectric power generation, job creation and environmental quality provide a common plank for debate as the states grapple with the political realities, of altering the flow of various rivers. Several water tribunals have been formed and judgments pronounced in many river basin disputes but solutions have been few. In the case of Cauvery, the problem has persisted for more than a century. There are also many court cases pending at local levels as regards the uses of water, and this affects the livelihoods of many.

> ➢ **Politics of Water Disputes**

Water remains virtually a state subject vide **entry 17** in the **State List**. The centre has not utilised its authority to legislate on this matter vide entry 56 in the Union List according to **Article 262** of the Constitution. While the Ravi-Beas and Satlej–Yamuna Canal Link remain unresolved, there are cases which have been resolved. Alan Richards and Nirvikar Singh attribute the main reason for their resolution to negotiations. The tribunals in this case proved ineffective. But regarding the Cauvery Water dispute and the Ravi-Beas water dispute both the negotiations and the tribunals proved ineffective.

Besides the ineffective awards of the tribunals, the centre's unwillingness to utilise entry 17 in the Union List according to **Article 262** of the Constitution to legislate on water disputes, political considerations are the major hindrances in resolving them. The possibility of resolution of the issue is viewed in a contradictory manner. While one state considers it advantageous to it the other sees its interosts, as against its interests.

Any inter-state water dispute has its repercussions on the politics and people in neighbouring states. It has ethnic implications. As some linguistic and ethnic groups live within states which have disputes over the sharing of water, these ethnic groups also get drawn into violent riots. In **1992 the Cauvery water dispute** between Tamil Nadu and Karnatka led to anti-Tamil riots in Tamil Nadu. This had further repercussion in the state politics of the two states. While the Tamil groups demanded protection of their ethnic and linguistic identities, the Karnataka political leadership in general opposed giving water to Tamil Nadu. They said that there was no surplus water that could be given to Tamil Nadu.

THE BOUNDARY DISPUTES

The longstanding tension between the states of Maharashtra and Karnataka over the rightful ownership of the district of Belgaun, between Punjab and Haryana over the Abohar-Fazilka Tehsil or about several such cases involving two or more states. Infact, the creation of certain new states in the last few years–Uttaranchal, Jharkhand and Chhattisgarh for instance-was partly a recognition of the longstanding problem of contesting territorial boundaries. The issue is complex and vexed and its roots can be traced to India's colonial past.

> ➢ **A Colonial Legacy**

India, as we known it today, has traversed a chequered path from ancient times. The boundaries of its constituent geographical units have been continually changing. However, till the advent of the British it was not really a nation-state, as the term is understood and the frequent changes in territorial limits did not amount to much. The British, in pursuance of their own colonial agenda, set about defining and redefining geographical limits and this created problems, the lingering effects of which can be felt till today. These effects can be felt even internationally. For **example**, India's boundary disputes with Pakistan, China and Bangladesh.

This was essentially because our colonial masters were guided primarily by the consideration of facile governance and towards this end, they focused on administrative aspects rather than linguistic/cultural etc.

unification. The result was a mismatch between people's personal identities and the territories they inhabited. It was left to the central government of free India to rectify the damage caused by the British colonialists' sectarianism and short sightedness.

➤ Territorial Issue in the Post - Colonial Period

The central legislature – the Parliament – was empowered by the constitution 'to create new states or merge old states or parts of such states or alter their boundaries in future'. It may interest you to know that even during the tenure of the Constituent Assembly the specially created and convened body to draft free India's constitution-demands had been raised for a linguistic reorganisation of states, the assumption being that linguistic commonality is an index of a common culture and thus, states created on the basis of a common/ unifying language would be more homogenous and thus, conducive to effective governance. However, at that time, the founding fathers of the Constitution had postponed the demand for a linguistic reconfiguration on the ground that the newly formed country might plunge into chaos and turmoil. But soon after independence, the government of Jawaharlal Nehru – India's first Prime-Minister changed tacks. Possibly, it felt that there was no other way out.

Thus, it had to cope with the agitation for an Andhra state. According to the Linguistic Provinces Commission, the demand first raised in the cosastal regions of Andhra had become "a passion" and "ceased to be a matter of reason". Immediately after the First General Election (1951-52), the Andhra Pradesh Provincial Congress Committee (APCC) had passed a resolution for the creation of a separate Telugu speaking state. The then Madras state also came in the picture and the State Congress Committee there endorsed the creation of the proposed new state.

The creation of Andhra gave a fillip to the demand for a further linguistic reorganisation of states and the government ended up setting a three member States Reorganisation Commission in 1953 to look into the whole question of altering old/creating new state boundaries. The Commission submitted its report in 1955 and its major recommendation was the creation of new states in the South of the country. In 1956, the States Reorganisation Act was passed.

But from the 1960s onwards, the process of creation of new states got going. Thus, in 1960 itself the state of Bombay was partitioned to create the new states of Maharashtra and Gujarat. Similarly, in 1966 the new state of Punjab was created. We have already mentioned about the creation of the new states of Uttaranchal, Chhattisgarh and Jharkhand in recent times. It is important to mention here that during the period, the northeastern part of the country also underwent a major reorganisation. Thus, in 1963 the state of Nagaland and in 1972, the state of Meghalaya were created.

> ### An Example Belgaun Dispute: An Example

The district of Belgaun is currently located in the state of Karnataka (North-West) and borders Maharashtra as well as Goa. Approximately, 20% of the local populace is of Maharashtrian origin.

The roots of the Marathi-Kannadiga conflict over the district of Belgaun- as with many such conflicts - are directly attributable to the linguistic reorganisation of states in India after independence. Belgaun district consists of a mixed population of Marathi and Kannada speakers. After the formation of Maharashtra state, some parts where Kannada was spoken got transferred to Karnataka, but some Marathi speaking pockets were also transferred to Karnataka. Belgaum is one such district which has a population of Marathi and Kannada speakers. The cause of these displaced Maharashtrians has been spearheaded for more than four decades by the Maharashtra Ekikaran Samiti (MES). It has stood for transferring selected Marathi dominated areas of Belgaun (especially the town of Belgaun) to Maharashtra. The case of the MES is **based on two premises**:

i) Language and ethnicity – the criteria for the reorganisation of states.

ii) Alleged or real discrimination against Marathis in education and employment (particularly government service).

The Kannadigas, especially those resident of Belgaun Town, lay claims to the area on historical grounds. Mainly, that the town of Belgaun had always been an intrinsic pat of a district that was chiefly Kannada speaking.

A third and no less significant factor in the longstanding conflict has been the political compromise effected by the then central government.

That is, some Kannada speaking districts of the old Hyderabad state were given to the new state of Andhra Pradesh in exchange for Belgaun being given to Karnataka.

13.2: IGNOU Book Exercise – Solved

1) Contextualise the water and territorial disputes in relation to federalism in India.

Answer by India Ebook: Read the Whole Concept and Write in Beief.

2) Analyse the factors for the persistence of inter-state water disputes.

Answer by India Ebook: Major conflict or disagreement over inter-state river waters in India is due to desire of initial allocation of property right over water, desperation of water scarce areas, political ambitions, historical troubles and non performance of existing laws.

Why interstate water disputes are looming:

i) The most prominent problem faced by interstate dispute is that it do not have any effective authority for the implementation of the order of the tribunal. The tribunal can only give an award but cannot enforce its implementation. It also don't have any powers of punishment for contempt.

ii) The awards of these tribunals, although supposedly final & binding, have been challenged in the courts. The judicial process is essentially an long process which further delay the dispute. e.g., Cauvery water dispute.

iii) Concerns of environmental impacts, rehabiliation measures have not been effectively assessed.

iv) Water is an emotional issue as large parts of the country are dominated by agriculture. This issues has been frequently used for mobilization of people for political purposes.

v) Scarcity of Water in certain areas.

Possible Solution

a) Article 263 of the Indian Constitution envisages establishing an Inter-State Council. The council provides a forum for discussion on complex public policy and governance issues having a bearing on centre-state relations or with an inter-state dimensions.

b) River Basin Organisation can be set up under the River Boards Act of 1956, legislated under Article 56 of the Union List. These are empowered to regulate and develop inter-state rivers and their basins. The board must comprise of members with expertise in fields such as irrigation, water and soil conservation and finance.

c) There should be proper mediation that employs a neutral person or persons to facilitate negotiations between the disputing parties so as to arrive at mutually acceptable solution. This process was successful when World Bank becomes a mediator for handling water dispute between India and Pakistan.

d) It has been recommended by the Sarkaria Commission that the tribunal awards should be equated with the status of the decree of the Supreme Court. Appeals to the court in large number to the court reflects the failure of the government in the handling water related disputes.

e) To develop the machinery for settlement of inter-state river Water disputes, Section 4 of the Act must be amended setting a time frame for constituting the Tribunal by the Centre.

3) Write a note on inter-state territorial disputes.

Answer by India Ebook: The longstanding tension between the states of Maharashtra and Karnataka over the rightful ownership of the district of Belgaun, between Punjab and Haryana over the Abohar-Fazilka Tehsil or about several such cases involving two or more states. Infact, the creation of certain new states in the last few years–Uttaranchal, Jharkhand and Chhattisgarh for instance-was partly a recognition of the longstanding problem of contesting territorial boundaries. The issue is complex and vexed and its roots can be traced to India's colonial past.

India, as we known it today, has traversed a chequered path from ancient times. The boundaries of its constituent geographical units have been continually changing. However, till the advent of the British it was not really a nation-state, as the term is understood and the frequent changes in territorial limits did not amount to much. The British, in pursuance of their own colonial agenda, set about defining and redefining geographical limits and this created problems, the lingering effects of which can be felt till today. These effects can be felt even internationally. For **example**, India's boundary disputes with Pakistan, China and Bangladesh.

After independence, the creation of Andhra gave a fillip to the demand for a further linguistic reorganisation of states and the government ended up setting a three member States Reorganisation Commission in 1953 to look into the whole question of altering old/creating new state boundaries. The Commission submitted its report in 1955 and its major recommendation was the creation of new states in the South of the country. In 1956, the States Reorganisation Act was passed.

But from the 1960s onwards, the process of creation of new states got going. Thus, in 1960 itself the state of Bombay was partitioned to create the new states of Maharashtra and Gujarat. Similarly, in 1966 the new state of Punjab was created. We have already mentioned about the creation of the new states of Uttaranchal, Chhattisgarh and Jharkhand in recent times. It is important to mention here that during the period, the northeastern part of the country also underwent a major reorganisation. Thus, in 1963 the state of Nagaland and in 1972, the state of Meghalaya were created.

13.3: IGNOU Past 6 Attempts Question – Solved

June 2019: Examine the factors for the persistence of interstate water disputes.

Dec 2020: Briefly discuss the nature of Inter-State disputes in India.

June 2021: What are the reasons for the persistence of inter-state water disputes ? Elaborate.

Dec 2021: Examine the reasons for the persistence of Inter-State water disputes.

Answer by India Ebook: Same as Q.2 of Above.

June 2020: Write short note: (a) Constitutional mechanisms for resolution of inter-state conflicts

Dec 2021: Briefly describe the Constitutional mechanisms for resolution of Inter-State conflicts in India.

Answer by India Ebook: Refer Concepts Above.

Dec 2020: Write short note: (a) Politics of Water Disputes between States.

Answer by India Ebook: Refer Concepts Above.

14. PATTERNS OF COMMUNAL POLITICS

14.1: One Shot Concepts

INTRODUCTION

Following independence the political elite in India were faced with the task of entering the legislative bodies. They needed to mobilise people to get their political support. This need for political mobilisation modivated them to search for the issues in the society. These issues were of the two kind socio-economic and emotional. The former included the basic needs of employment, education and basic infrastructure. The latter included the issue of building India into a nation-state as well issues relating to the markers with which people identify by birth — religion, language, tribe or caste. The mobilisation on the basis of caste, religion, language, or the tribe has been taking place in India indifferent ways. Religion has been one of the most important forces of the communal mobilisation in India.

WHAT IS COMMUNAL POLITICS?

Communal politics is a South Asian expression for what is globally described as ethnic or sectarian politics. Such politics is based on a belief that religion forms the basis of a common identity; that members of a particular religious community have the same economic, political and social interests. In other words, communal politics works on the belief that each religious community is distinct from the other in its religious, cultural practices, lifestyles and value systems which become the basis of differences in socio-economic interests between these communities. In the absence of shared interests it is only distrust and suspicion that tends to define the relationship between different communities. Communal politics generates mutual distrust between religious communities. This feeling of distrust often leads to violence, which has a place of importance for communal politics, as it deepend the mutual suspicion and hatreds which fuelled violence in the first place. Communal violence thus, leads to communal polarisation of society and hence, helps in the expansion of communal politics.

Communal politics in this sense is primarily a form of politics, which mobilises a particular religious community for political power. It is the exploitation of religious differences for political gains. Communal politics may also take the form of highlighting the communitarian interests of a religious group without necessarily generating hatred towards any other community. What is important about communal politics is that it is not driven by any religious or spiritual issue, but secular interests, which can range from bargaining for jobs, educational concessions, political patronage, separate representation or control over institutions of governance. Crucial forcommunal politics is a feeling of oneness within a religious community as also a sense of cultural difference between communities.

Communal politics, as distinguished from **communal violence** (or communal riots), is a particular approach to politics which is practiced at a sustained level. Communal violence involves incidents of violence between two religious communities. It can be sporadic in nature and mainly forms a law and order issue to be handled on the spot for restoring peace and calm. Though communal politics does not need immediate police intervention, it has much more damaging implications over the long term. It breeds feelings of suspicion between religious communities and also raises the frequency of violence which in turn sustains communal politics.

HOW AND WHEN DID COMMUNAL POLITICS ARISE IN INDIA?

Communal politics arose in British India mainly as a bargaining medium for positions of economic privilege and social status under colonial rule. As such, the early communal politics was in the nature of competition for government patronage, jobs, educational concessions and political positions, and was not necessarily something that generated communal animosity. The politics of Syed Ahmad Khan and the Aligarh school can be placed in this category. This politics was more of an interest-oriented politics rather than one based strictly on ideology. Its prime concern was the upward socio-economic mobility of the Muslim community.

The relations of both the Muslim and Hindu communal politics with the Indian National Congress remained tense. From the very beginning this politics tried to keep itself consciously away from the Congress-led nationalist movement, though often it was overwhelmed by circumstances and had to join the secularliberal anti-colonial movement.

It also happened that in the early 20th century anti-colonial mobilisation often occurred on religious issues and brought people into the nationalist struggle as religious communities. For example, the Akali agitations against the corrupt, British-supported Gurudwara managements between 1919 and 1926 brought the Sikh community into the nationalist struggle. This brave and relentless agitaion against ruthless Mahants eventually led to a strong movement against British rule itself. The Khilafat agitation against the British in 1920-21 to restore the Caliphate in Turkey—once again a religious issue—drew this time the Muslims to the freedom struggle.

The British, to weaken the nationalist movement, encouraged communal and separatist politics and tried to strengthen the impression that Congress was a Hindu organisation. This was in line with their policy of '**divide and rule**'. The British government's support to separatist politics together with the indigenous elite's hankering for material privileges gave way in the 1930s to the idea that Hindus and Muslims constitute two separate and hostile nations.

The **Congress** was **committed** to **Hindu-Muslim unity** and building a strong front against the British. It also made attempts to build some kind of a socio-economic programme for an independent India. There existed within the Congress a strong Hindu right wing, but it remained marginal and was not able to dominate the all-encompassing, all-India character of the Congress. The fear of the 'Hindu' character of the Congress was exaggerated by the British government as well as by the Muslim League to strengthen communal separatism. Though the Congress was wedded to non-communal politics, there was no conceptual clarity within the party about what a secular state policy should be.

The concluding years of the British rule in India witnessed the most gruesome Hindu-Muslim riots. The 'Direct Action Day' called by the Muslim League in 1946 set off large scale violence in Calcutta that continued for several months. Town after town witnessed killing sprees. Violence in Bengal and Bihar spread to the Punjab and NWFP. This was a time when the non-separatist Muslim leadership was completely overshadowed and popular support began to shift to the Muslim League, a fact which goes on to shows the importance of violence for communal politics. Partition of the sub-continent took a further toll upon Hindu-Muslim relations. Communal killings whose number touched one million—and the accompanying displacement inflicted deep wounds on the national psyche and formed the basis of communal politics in independent India.

WHY DOES COMMUNAL POLITICS THRIVE?

An economy which is marked by slow and haphazard growth, rising levels of unemployment, unmanageable levels of poverty, low literacy levels, falling health standards, etc., is prone to mobilisations based on community, religion, caste and sect. A society facing economic hardships—poverty, hunger and unemployment—is more likely to support community based politics. Uneven economic development and distribution, in terms of region as well as social groups, works to the advantage of communal politics.

Two reasons can be given to explain the differences of wealth. First the successive governments have failed to bring about a just distribution of resources and to provide minimum access to education and health. Second, the religio-cultural reasons are responsible for the differences in wealth. Communal politics uses the second explanation and advances itself. It also constructs the exploitation of a community by another, or regions for the basis wordiness, rich in reality might not even exist.

Moreover, it is **much easier for the ruling elite** to **mobilise people on narrow communal lines**. Such mobilisations are short-cuts to power. Improving the economic status of the masses requires a will and commitment over long term. This commitment is something which can eventually pose a challenge to the dominant political and economic interests. The rate of economic development remains painfully slow, not least due to the massive corruption involving the political leadership. Often, the state resorts to cutting down on welfare schemes meant for the people. Resources are withdrawn from education and health sectors, employment generation schemes are frozen and workers retrenched from public sector undertakings to meet the fiscal crises of the state.

Communal politics is of great utility in breaking any popular opposition to these policies. In such situations communal politics helps channelise the anger of the people away from the leadership responsible for their economic underdevelopment towards other communities.

Lastly, often communal riots have been instigated to eliminate a business rival and to take over coveted property. In an event of economic competition, traders and entrepreneurs of a particular community often use communal politics and violence to smother competition from business rivals of a different community.

COMMUNAL POLITICS AND THE INTERPRETATION OF HISTORY Book Q.2

Communal politics to be able to operate smoothly, relies heavily upon the past. It is dependent upon a certain interpretation of history and its selective appropriation distortions, constructions, decontextualisation and selective picking and choosing form the baggage of communalisation of history, something indispensable for communal politics. As such an imagined past is created to serve communal needs. As such an imagined past is created to serve needs of communal politics.

For instance, **Hindu communalism** operates with a view of history where certain eternally noble characteristics are attributed to Hindus, such as tolerance, respectful of other's religious beliefs, spirituality, unmindful of material desires, etc. These attributes are said to be in full bloom during the ancient period of the history of India, a period interpreted as one of glory and prosperity for the Hindu nation (the 'nation' is also attributed an imagined antiquity). This ancient era is considered Hindu heritage which needs to be revived.

The entry of the Muslims is said to have spoilt this period of calm, prosperity and creativity. With the entry of Muslims India is said to have embarked on the second phase of its history, the medieval period, an era of darkness. This was an era, so it is propagated, of Muslim fanaticism and destruction, — the Muslims were driven by the sole religious aim of conversions and destruction of the places of worship of the Hindus. In this history, Muslims are unflinchingly attached the traits of fanaticism, iconoclasts, marauders and murderers.

Conversely, for the Muslim communalists, it is the medieval era which needs to be looked up to. It was a period when Muslim power was at the helm — a glorious time of Muslim rule. This marking of historical periods on the basis of religion of the rulers is in itself ahistorical putting in doubt this entire exercise. It is a history, which does not even remotely resemble the complex currents and cross-currents that make up the historical process.

An oft-repeated instance of Muslim 'fanaticism' is destruction of places of worship. What is conveniently forgotten is that the destruction of places of worship was not always due to religious fanaticism and it was not only the rulers of the Muslim faith who indulged in such activity. Often, political and socio-economic factors were responsible for the destruction of places of worship and also their conversions into rival shrines. This was not only peculiar to India, but occurred in other societies as well. Such destructions were assertions of political power and also ways of replenishing dry treasuries.

Communal politics thus breaks up history into simplified phases which besides giving a distorted picture of the past is also communal in nature. Moreover, religious prejudice rather than an objective view of history forms the basis of historic explanation. Here, religion and religious conflict are given a centrality and their role exaggerated to such an extent that even simple rivalries over secular issues are given a religious interpretation.

COMMUNAL POLITICS AND COMMUNAL VIOLENCE TODAY
Book Q.4

Over the years, as the economic hardships have grown, the politics of the country has turned increasingly towards communal issues for political mobilisation. Most often this has resulted in communal violence. Violence is important for communal politics for it leads to communalisation of society and results in a polarisation, which brings votes and political power. Therefore, communal riots are not sudden outbursts of religious conflicts.

Communal politics openly resorts to communal mobilisation for political ends. There is also a politics which opportunistically resorts to communal mobilisation for short term electoral gains. In the first category are groups like the VHP, the Shiv Sena, the Muslim League, the Majlis-e-Ittehadul Muslimeen, etc. In the second are parties like the Congress-I, the Trinamool Congress, the Telegu Desam, the Samata Party, etc.

The politics of **Ram-janma-bhoomi** has been a prime contributor to the electoral fortunes of the **BJP**. The Lok Sabha strength of the BJP went up from 2 seats in the 1984 election to 88 seats, in the 1989 elections and in the 1991 elections to 120 seats. It is this dependence of the BJP on the Ramjanmabhoomi movement which prevents it from dealing firmly with communal violence and politics despite being in power.

During the **Gujarat violence (2002)**, Muslims and their property were systematically targeted. In four days—28th February to 3rd March 2003—600 Muslims had been killed, though Amnesty International puts the number as 2000. More than 2 lakh Muslims were displaced, their homes looted and burnt. The number of Hindus who were displaced was 10,000.

The role of the police in communal violence needs to be taken into account also. From every major incident of communal violence in the country, what has almost invariably emerged is the partisan role of the police. The communalised character of the police has been more than evident. The police through its partisanship has helped communal politics and in fact has played the role of an oppressive bureaucracy in the service of the ruling class well.

During the **1992-93 Mumbai riots**, police used excessive force against and systematically refused to register their complaints against Hindu mobsters. The same was the story in Gujarat in 2002. The Muslims not only had to face the Hindu mobsters, many a times led by local VHP-Bajrang Dal supporters, but also the police. In Gujarat in 2002, the police did all that it was not expected to do and did not act where it should have taken action. The police directed the mobsters to Muslim homes, was a mute spectator to their killings, fired at Muslims, took part in looting their property, and did not register complaints of affected Muslims against their attackers. On February 28, 40 men shot dead near the Bapunagar police station were all Muslims, shot on the head and chest, while trying to defend themselves from a 3000 strong mob.

PATTERNS OF PRESENT DAY COMMUNAL POLITICS

Book Q.3

These happenings reveal some significant facts about communal politics after the emergence of Hindutva as a major ideological force on the political scene.

One, communalism has acquired an openness, a legitimacy and mass reach comparable to, and surpassing, what the Muslim League achieved in British India. Communal politics in the early decades of Independent India needed a screen from behind which it operated. The reach of Hindu communalism has spread, which is partly attributable to the first point discussed above, that is, the majoritarian religio-cultural understanding of democracy.

Two, present day communal politics, in its Hindu communal form, challenges the very foundations of democracy in India. It calls for the formation of a Hindu state and challenges the basic principles of equal citizenship, secularism, religious tolerance and religious freedoms — the foundations of a plural Indian polity. Hindutva has brought about this fundamental change in communalism post-late 1980s.

Three, in independent India, minority communal politics has not been able to survive the onslaught of Hindu politics. Earlier, minority and majority communal politics used to breed on each other to consolidate their spheres of influence and also, the Muslim League had considerable political clout. But, in independent India, Muslim politics, as an ideological force, has been pushed to an insignificant fringe.

Four, Muslim communal politics (in its communitarian form) is regionally specific. There are scattered pockets of its incluence that do not have any connection with each other. For example, the politics of MIM in Hyderabad, of the Muslim League in Kerala, of some leaders in Uttar Pradesh, etc., is regionally localised with little possibility of collaboration.

Five, Hindu communalism is ideologically much stronger than Muslim communalism, and this strength comes from its ability to identify with Indian nationalism. Hindu communalism's trait to conveniently slip into claims of Indian nationalism is something which Muslim communalism can never achieve, rather it, like all other minority nationalisms, is always in danger of being branded separatist and anti-national. Hindu communalism's ideological expression is revealed in Hindutva which has a geographic uniformity and unity.

Six, Hindu communal politics has got an added force from the way world politics itself has moved. The identification of Islam with global terrorism at the hands of the neo-imperialist forces after the 11th September 2001 attacks on the World Trade Centre towers in New York has come as a big political and ideological support to the Hindu communal forces. This has led them to intensify their politics of hate against the Muslims in India for a further political expansion. The activities of extremist groups like **Al Qaida** at the international level, and of the Mumbai underworld at the national level has made matters convenient for Hindutva forces in India to identify Muslims as anti-national and terrorists.

14.2: IGNOU Book Exercise – Solved

1) What is communal politics? Discuss the relationship between communal politics and economic development.

Answer by India Ebook: Communal politics in this sense is primarily a form of politics, which mobilises a particular religious community for political power. It is the exploitation of religious differences for political gains. Communal politics may also take the form of highlighting the communitarian interests of a religious group without necessarily generating hatred towards any other community.

Communal politics generates mutual distrust between religious communities. This feeling of distrust often leads to violence, which has a place of importance for communal politics, as it deepend the mutual suspicion and hatreds which fuelled violence in the first place. Communal violence thus, leads to communal polarisation of society and hence, helps in the expansion of communal politics.

Today in India we see the **Hindu communalism**, which is ideologically **much stronger than Muslim communalism**, and this strength comes from its ability to identify with Indian nationalism.

RELATIONSHIP BETWEEN COMMUNAL POLITICS & ECONOMIC DEVELOPMENT

An economy which is marked by **slow and haphazard growth**, rising levels of **unemployment**, unmanageable levels of **poverty**, **low literacy** levels, **falling health** standards, etc., is <u>**prone to mobilisations based on community, religion, caste and sect.**</u> A society facing economic hardships—poverty, hunger and unemployment—is more likely to support community based politics. Uneven economic development and distribution, in terms of region as well as social groups, works to the advantage of communal politics.

Two reasons can be given to explain the differences of wealth. **First** the successive governments have failed to bring about a just distribution of resources and to provide minimum access to education and health. **Second**, the religio-cultural reasons are responsible for the differences in wealth. Communal politics uses the second explanation and advances itself. It also constructs the exploitation of a community by another, or regions for the basis wordiness, rich in reality might not even exist.

2) What kind of interpretation of history does communal politics rely on?

Answer by India Ebook: Read the 1 Shot Concept Above.

3) What are the patterns of communal politics in India today?

Answer by India Ebook: Read the 1 Shot Concept Above.

4) Spell out the necessity of communal violence for communal politics?

Answer by India Ebook: Read the 1 Shot Concept Above.

14.3: IGNOU Past 6 Attempts Question – Solved

June 2019: Examine the pattern of communal politics in contemporary India.

Answer by India Ebook: Almost same as **Q.1** above.

15. ASSERTION OF DALITS AND BACKWARD CASTES

Introduction
Socio-Economic Conditions
- ➢ Dalits
- ➢ Backward Castes
Assertion of Dalits
- ➢ The Republican Party of India
- ➢ The Dalit Panther
- ➢ The Bahujan Samaj Party
- ➢ Left and Dalit Question
Assertion of Backward Classes
- ➢ North India
- ➢ South India
- ➢ Organisations of Backward Castes

15.1: One Shot Concepts

INTRODUCTION

During the past few decades there has been an assertion of the dalits and backward classes in India. The latter are also known as the other backward classes (OBCs). Through such assertions these groups have seek to strive for social and cultural autonomy, self-respect and dignity, and demand a share in the political power. They are playing very dominant role in politics of several states. In the recent past they have become a formidable components of the power structure in the national politics.

SOCIO-ECONOMIC CONDITIONS Book Q.1

➢ Dalits

Dalits is a term generally used for the ex-untouchable castes, which have been identified as the Scheduled Castes by our constitution. They form a large number of castes and have been involved in the low ranking occupations like leather work, scavenging and agricultural labourers.

Reservation in the educational and political institutions have given rise to the emergence of an articulate group among them. This group articulates their problems. This also indicates towards a process social transformation, which has taken place in India. But the social transformation has shown uneven patterns in the country. In large areas of the country, especially the rural areas, dalits continue to face indignities and humiliations. Despite the comprehensive provisions in the Constitution of India, the fight against dalits' discrimination is yet to be won. Dalits continue to suffer from the menace till date.

Article 17 of the Constitution had abolished "Untouchability". The provisions of affirmative action contained in the Constitution have become redundant in some cases. The entire private sector is under no obligation to do social justice to dalits. Dalits' demand for reservation in the private sector faces stiff opposition from several powerful and articulate groups.

➢ Backward Castes

Backward Castes are also known as backward classes or the Other Backward Classes (OBCs). Our constitution identifies those social groups as OBCs, which are educationally and socially backward. This categorisation includes those groups among the OBCs, which are not necessarily backward politically or economically. That is why a large number of the castes identified as OBCs are quite influencial in politics and economy, especially agriculture in different states of India. Unlike dalits, OBCs is a more differentiated category. It includes the intermediary land owning castes as well as the landless service castes. The land owning middle or intermediary castes are mainly Jats, Yadavs, Gujars, Lodhs, Kurmies in the north India, Marathas and Patels in Maharastra and Gujarat and Reddies, Kammas, Vokaliggas and Lingayats in South India. It is these castes which are the most assertive among the OBCs.

ASSERTION OF DALITS Book Q.2

Post-independence period in India has seen **assertion of dalits in India**. This assertion can be divided into three phases –

- the phase of Republican Party of India;
- the phase of Dalit Panther and
- the phase of Bahujan – Samaj Party (BSP).

Since this assertion took place after the death of Ambedkar all these phases belong to the post-Ambedkar dalit movement. The focus of dalit movement in the preceding period had been on the temple entry, restoration of self-respect, and getting reservation for the dalits in the political and government institutions. The post-Ambedkar dalit movement took the multiple forms - socio-cultural, economic and political. Due to their assertion dalits have been able to get the recognition as a distinct social and political group. Their assertion is reflected through various ways i.e., foundation of social, cultural and political organisations, conversion to other religion and increasing political participation.

A number of factors account for the assertion of dalits. The most important of these are the rise of an educated and articulate group among them, the expansion of mass media and most importantly the impact of ideas and life of Dr. B.R. Ambedkar on them.

> ### The Republican Party of India

A few years before his death Dr B.R. Ambedkar founded the Republican Party of India (RPI). This party aimed at amelioration of the socio-economic conditions of dalits and the poorer classes and to enable them to capture political power. After Ambedkar's death the RPI was strengthened by an emergent educated middle class of dalits. The RPI became popular mainly in Uttar Pradesh and Maharastra in the 1950s and 1960s. In Uttar Pradesh it even contested elections in 1960s and became a force to reckon with. In UP the RPI forged an alliance of dalits, Muslims and the OBCs. But it lost its popularity after 1960s as some of its prominent leaders got accommodated in the Congress party. In Maharastra the RPI was split into several groups, marked by ideological and personal differences. It is important to note that the RPI worked among dalits on two fronts – political and cultural.

> ### The Dalit Panther

Influenced by Marxism Ambedkarism and Negro literature a group of dalit intellectuals founded Dalit Panther in Maharastra in 1972. It was basically a movement of dalit intellectuals, which contributed to generating consciousness among dalits to a significant extent. It attacked the Hindu Caste system through literary activities, debates and discussion in homes, offices and public places. An incident was the main cause for setting up the Dalit Panther. Dalit Panther was named after the Black Panther of USA.

➤ The Bahujan Samaj Party

The rise of BSP in last two decades of 20th Century in north India, and becoming Chief Minister of its leader Mayawati thrice in Uttar Pradesh symbolises the empowerment of dalits in India. The rise of the BSP is part of the process of dalit empowerment, which started in the postindependence period. Founded by Kashi Ram, on April 14, 1984 the Bahujan Samaj Party aims to empower the majroty section of the society or bahujan samaj – dalits, OBCs tribals and minorities.

➤ Left and Dalit Question

Dalit assertion has also taken place through the mobilisation by the left especially the in Bihar, Andhra Pradesh and parts of some other states. The naxalites have taken up the issues of dual exploitation of dalits – caste exploitation and class exploitation involving issues related to selfrespect, exploitation of woman, wages and land reforms. The naxalites are not averse to using the violent means to get their demands conceded. PWG (People's War Group), Party Unity, Indian People's Front are some of the naxalite organisations, which work towards dalit assertion. They are countered by the high castes and landlords' organisations like 'Lorik Sena' or 'Bhoomi Sena' in Bihar. The major left parties – the CPI(M) and the CPI did not feel, till recently, special the need to mobilise dalits on the caste question. For them dalits were constituents of the poorer classes, which face economic exploitation.

ASSERTION OF BACKWARD CLASSES
Book Q.3

➤ North India

Assertion of backward castes in North India is basically assertion of middle or intermediary castes, i.e., Jats, Yadavs, Gujars, Kurmies, Lodhs, etc. in Uttar Pradesh, Bihar, Rajasthan, and Haryana. The lower backwards – the artisans and service castes do not show the kind of assertion which the intermediary castes have shown. The credit to mobilise the backward castes in north India during the post-independence period actually goes to Charan Singh. Though his caste, Jat was not categorised as an OBCs in Uttar Pradesh till 2002, he identified himself with other backward classes like Yadavs, Kurmies, Lodhs and Gujars.

Backward classes formed an important section in the Janata Party. Issues of backward classes, rural sector and agriculture got special focus of the Janata Party government during 1977-1980. One result of the backward castes' assertion was appointment of Mandal Commission, for identifying the backward classes. The implementation of Mandal Commission Report by V.P. Singh's government in 1989 shows the culmination of the process of backward caste assertion. These developments indicate towards the assertion of the backward classes. The backward classes are accommodated in different political parties: some parties like the Rashtriya Janata Dal in Bihar and Samajwadi Party in Uttar Pradesh are largely identified with the backward classes.

➢ **South India**

Backward castes' assertion in south Indian States - Tamil Nadu, Karnataka and Maharashtra started much earlier to that in north India. It had its root in the non-Brahmin movement or the self-respect movement which was led by E V Ramaswami Naickar popularly known as Periyar in the 1920s and 1930s. The legacy of Periyar was carried forward by C.M. Annadurai and M. Karunanidhi and several of his followers. It aimed to demolish the Brahmins' domination in culture and public institutions. It attacked cultural symbols identified with Hinduism or Brahminism, preached atheism against the belief in God. The backward classes' aspirations and ideology were articulated through the political parties like the Justice Party, the DMK (Dravida Munnetra Kaghgam), ADMK (Anna Dravida Munneba Kaghgam) and AIDMK (All India Anna Dravida Munnetra Kaghgam).

➢ **Organisations of Backward Castes**

A large number of backward class associations appeared in the post–independence period. Marc Gallenter observed that by 1954, there were 88 organisations in India, which articulated the interests of the backward classes. The most important of these existed in North India. These were UP Backward Classes Federation and Bihar State Backward Classes Federation. These two organisations merged on 26 January 1950 to form All India Backward Classes Federation (AIBCF) by the efforts of Punjab Rao Deshmukh.

The AIBCF had split into two groups – one adhering to the Congress ideology and another Lohiaite socialism. The former was represented by Punjab Rao Deshmuk and the latter by R L Chandpuri. R L Chandpuri formed Indian National Backward Classes Federation (INBCF) on 10 November, 1957. These organisations sought to get the reservation for the OBCs and empower the them in order to overthrow the 'Brahmin-Baniya Raj'. The organisations contributed to the rise of consciousness of the OBCs. This consciousness, coupled with the result of land reforms and adequate numerical strength led to the assertion of the OBCs.

15.2: IGNOU Book Exercise - Solved

1) Discuss the socio-economic condition of dalits and OBCs in India.

Answer by India Ebook: Read the 1 Shot Concept Above.

2) What factors have contributed to the **assertion of dalits**?

Answer by India Ebook: Read the 1 Shot Concept Above.

3) Write a note on the assertion of backward castes in India.

Answer by India Ebook: Read the 1 Shot Concept Above.

15.3: IGNOU Past 6 Attempts Question - Solved

June 2019: Describe different forms of Dalit assertion since the 1980s.

Answer by India Ebook: Almost same as **Q.2** above.

June 2020: Examine the impact of assertion of Dalit politics in India.

Dec 2020: Examine the factors contributing to the rise of Dalit and Backward Classes in Indian politics.

Answer by India Ebook: Refer Concept above.

June 2021: Analyse the impact of Dalit assertion on politics and society in India.

Answer by India Ebook: Refer Concept above.

16. LINGUISTIC AND ETHNIC MINORITIES IN STATE POLITICS

Introduction
Who are the Linguistic and Ethnic Minorities?
Linguistic Minorities and Politics
Ethnic Minorities and Politics

16.1: One Shot Concepts

INTRODUCTION

The linguistic and ethnic minorities occupy a significant place in democracy. Their empowerment in terms of participation in political processes, ability to avail of the distributive justice, security, freedom, equality, etc. is indicative of level of success of a democracy. In a multicultural and diverse society like India the multiple identities based on the diverse factors - caste, language, religion, race, culture, traditions, customs, etc. play significant role in impacting their place in democracy. The mobilisation, patronage, discrimination, in society and politics based on these markers form significant part of a democratic system.

WHO ARE THE LINGUISTIC AND ETHNIC MINORITIES?

A minority is a group of persons whose numbers are smaller than the number of another group. It is a relative term; a group is minority in comparison to the other group, which forms the majority. The basis of the minority status of a group or community could be a single marker or more, i.e, language, religion, culture, customs, traditions, race, economy, etc. The denomination of a community whether it a linguistic, religious or cultural minority or majority depends on the basis of factor with which the group or the community is identified. The scholars in India generally address a community of the basis of single marker - language, religion or region. They use ethnic and communal interchangeably. The Indian scholars generally consider that identity as ethnic which is formed by multiple factors - language, caste, religion, culture, customs, traditions, race, economy, etc.

There could be two levels of identification of the linguistic minorities - national and state/Union Territories. Even within the states there are again vertical and horizontal levels where the linguistic minorities exist.

At all India level the linguistic majority consists of Hindi speakers; other linguistic groups are linguistic minorities. But the linguistic groups which are minorities at the all India level are linguistic majorities in different states. The groups within the states which do not speak the language of majority are linguistic minorities. All states of India have more than one linguistic minorities. The formation of states in the basis of language did not remove the linguistic diversities from there.

There are 18 national languages, which are listed in the VIII Schedule of the Constitution. These are Assamese, Bengali, Gujarati, Hindi, Kannada, Kashmiri, Konkani, Malayalam, Marathi, Manipuri, Nepali, Oriya, Punjabi, Sanskrit, Sindhi, Tamil, Telugu and Urdu. Except Hindi, most of these languages are the principal languages in a single state. From these languages Hindi is expected to "draw" its vocabulary wherever necessary and primarily on Sanskrit and secondarily on other languages. Besides, there are hundreds of dialects and languages in different regions spoken by variety of communities within the states.

The significance of language as the basis of identity in India was recognised in the early 20th century when Congress had organised itself on the linguistic lines. But after independence Congress had shown its reluctance to organise states on the linguistic basis till the state reorganisation Commission made its recommendation for linguistic organisation of states. This too was in the wake of the death of a Gandhian, P. Sriramulu, from Andhra Pradesh as a result of the hunger strike demanding a Telugu state Andhra Pradesh, which was created in 1953. The reorganisation of the states on the linguistic basis in 1956, however, did not resolve the language question.

There is close a relationship between ethnicity and the linguistic identity. Some scholar do not differentiate between ethnicity, linguistic identify and communalism. A linguistic minority also shares multiple attributes among its members. In a mobilisation, which may be on a single factor, language, there is the collective mobilisation of the members of the linguistic groups. It is particularly so in the context of conflict between members of one linguistic group and those of another.

LINGUISTIC MINORITIES AND POLITICS   Book Q.2

Politics of linguistic minorities has principally been impacted by these factors: their perception of themselves and of the linguistic majorities, the attitude of the linguistic majorities towards them, and the linguistic majorities' perception of the linguistic minorities. The linguistic majorities in different states have demanded that the linguistic minorities accept the language of the majorities as medium of instruction in educational institutions and the official language. They have done it through the three or four language formula. The linguistic minorities have demanded protection of their language by demanding its inclusion in **VIII Schedule** of the Constitution. It must be noted that demand for recognition of language as an official language or its inclusion in the **VIII Schedule** is rarely made as an independent demand; it is one of the several demands.

There are a large number linguistic minorities in state of North-East India. The linguistic groups of the region can again be linked to the ethnic groups. The latter belong to two blocs of ethnic communities – the minorities indigenous groups which have not migrated from anywhere else outside the state, and those who have come from other states and settled there over the years in search of employment. The latter consist of minority multi-lingual groups. But the former consist of several single language minority groups. Assam is among the north-eastern states where the linguistic minorities have resisted the attempts of the linguistic majority to make its language as official and court language of all.

In Assam the principal linguistic conflict has been between the Assamese and the non-Assamese languages. When Assam was a composite state, i.e., before other states were carved of Assam, the conflict was between the Assamese on the one hand and the non-Assamese on the other. The latter included the Bengali, tribal languages, etc. But after formation of separates states out of Assam, especially Meghalaya in 1972, in Assam the main contradiction has been Bengalis and Assamese. Bengalis are a minority linguistic group in Brahmputra Valley and Assamese in Barak Valley. The Bengalis fear that introduction of Assamese as the official language would hamper the progress of Bengalis in Brahmputra Valley.

The Assamese-Bengali linguistic conflict in Assam can be traced back to the colonial policies. Within a few years of the occupation of Assam, the British made the Bengali as the official language. The Assamese had alleged that the British did so under the pressure of the Bengalis and it was discriminatory to them. They demanded that the Assamese be declared as an official and court language in Assam.

In Punjab also the linguistic issue got linked with the communal divide between Hindus and Sikhs during the Punjabi Suba movement of the 1960s. The Arya Samaj impacted the vision of non-Sikh Punjabis, who declared their language in the census enumeration as Hindi, though in reality it was Punjabi. It was mainly because of the communalisation of language and apprehension of Hindus that creation of separate states of Punjab excluding Haryana would reduce the Hindus to a minority community in Punjab. They felt by declaring Hindi as their mother-tongue would weaken the case for a separate state of Punjab.

ETHNIC MINORITIES AND POLITICS

In Indian context the ethnic identity is based on multiple factors unlike the linguistic identity, caste or communal identity which is based on a single attribute. Since ethnic identity is a relative identity, the politics of one ethnic group is formed in the light of the politics of another ethnic group. Again, the ethnic politics to a large extent depends on the real and imagined factors. All states of India have ethnic minorities. But it is generally in the states which have witnessed the political movements for self-determination movements - autonomy movements, secessionist movements, insurgencies, that their politics assumes special significance. A large number of states are witnessing such movements. But these are most assertive in north-east India, Jammu and Kashmir and Punjab.

In north-east Indian states there are two types of ethnic minorities - one, those who have been living there since centuries, those who have settled there as a result of migration from different parts of the country since nineteenth century, and who still continue to immigrate into the region. Each of the ethnic minority groups is further divided in their background, culture, etc. The immigrant settlers are further divided on the basis of their original states, the states from where they have migrated. But in times of their conflict with the majority ethnic groups, their differences get blurred and they tend to unite into an informal federation of ethnic minorities. Some of the most important examples of politics of ethnic minorities in north-east India are relatd to the Kukis in Nagaland, the Bodos, Santhals, Karbis in and non-tribals in Assam, and the non-tribals in Meghalaya.

The ethnic minorities sometime join the majority ethnic groups in a common pursuit. But after the movement has achieved its purpose, the dominant ethnic group does not give them their due and recognition. This gives them a feeling of neglect and discrimination. As a result they also demand autonomy for their ethnic group. The examples of Bodos and Karbi tribes of Assam are suitable in this context. These two tribes participated wholeheartedly in the six year long agitation against the foreigners in Assam led by AASU. But when the AGP formed the government, their problems were neglected by the AGP/ASSU which was dominated by the majority ethnic group of Assam. As a result the Bodo started an agitation demanding creation of a Bodoland. The same pattern is applicable to the Karbi tribe of the Karbi Anlong district.

The politics of ethnic minorities is decided by the course of the politics of ethnic majorities. Let us take the example of the ethnic majorities in case of Meghalaya. The ethnic minorities there are three local tribes - Khasis, Garos and Jaintias. The principal ethnic majorities are Bengalis, Nepalis, Biharis and Rajasthanis/Marwaris. Both groups of these ethnic communities joined together to demand a separate state of Meghalaya to be carved out of the then Assam in the 1960s. One of the principal reasons of their demand for a separate was their common grievance against making Assamese an official language, which they resisted as the ethnic majorities in Assam.

16.2: IGNOU Book Exercise – Solved

1) Discuss the characteristics of the linguistic minoities.

Answer by India Ebook: Read the 1 Shot Concept Above.

2) Identify and discuss the features of politics of linguistic minorities in Indian states.

Answer by India Ebook: Read the 1 Shot Concept Above.

3) Discuss the patterns of politics of ethnic minorities in Indian states.

Answer by India Ebook: Read the 1 Shot Concept Above.

16.3: IGNOU Past 6 Attempts Question – Solved

June 2019: Write a note on ethnic minorities in the country.   16

Answer by India Ebook: Refer Concept above.

June 2020: Comment on the nature and features of the politics of linguistic minorities in India.

Answer by India Ebook: Same as Q.1

Dec 2020: Write short note: (b) Linguistic Minorities and Politics .

Answer by India Ebook: Same as Q.1

17. STATE AUTONOMY MOVEMENTS IN INDIA

Introduction
Features of Autonomy Movements
The Indian Case
  - The Phase of Congress Hegemony: 1947 – 1977
  - The Janata Phase: 1977 – 1979
  - The Phase of Coalition Politics

17.1: One Shot Concepts

INTRODUCTION

The debate about the nature of the Indian federation as laid down in the constitution has gone on for about three decades now. The general trend of opinion has been to treat it as a federal constitution but with a very strong unitary bias. Its working during the last many decades has, however, been pronouncedly on unitary lines along with a steady encroachment on the powers of the states, which means that the Constitution provides mechanisms to the centre to encroach upon and curtail the rights and powers of the constituent states. In the 1990s in the era of coalition politics, which continues till now this process has been arrested though not reversed; all this due to the dependence of the Union governments on a variety of regional parties or the support of the Left. Moreover, provisions that make the centre all-powerful as against the states also tend to strengthen the executive as against the legislature. This process can in general terms be referred to as the centralisation of powers. This trend in turn gives rise to a counter movement on the part of the states to regain their powers.

FEATURES OF AUTONOMY MOVEMENTS   Book Q.1

One manifestation of the fight back on the part of the states has taken the shape of the movements talked off as the state autonomy movements. It is more than the fight for financial resources, which has been a constant refrain on the part of the states. This is so because the division of powers between the centre and states is such that balance of powers tends to be against the states. Without going into details let us take just an instance. All the powers to impose taxes on constantly expanding incomes, like excise and custom duties or the income tax, also known as the elastic sources of income are with the centre. Whereas sources of income which are static, also referred to as inelastic, with the exception of sales tax, are with the states.

Apart from the struggle for financial resources, the state autonomy movements have a political dimension, which gives them a distinct character. This dimension involves issues such as the question of the exercise of powers by the centre under Art.356, to dismiss the state government, appoint and remove governors, standing of the states within the federal structure, and such other questions. In all of these the centre exercises discretionary powers and the states are quite at the mercy of the centre.

One way of understanding both the process of centralisation of political power and the manifestation of the counter-tendency in the shape of the demands for 'State autonomy' is to look at it, at one level, through the consolidation and differentiation of the ruling classes like the capitalists and the landlords and how they seek to manage their contradictions and, at another level, to relate it to the growing democratic aspirations and concrete struggles of the common people, the working class, the peasantry and the other toiling people.

One very important consequence flows from the development of capitalism. The development of capitalism necessitates, as one of its conditions, the formation of larger markets for commodity production. This condition and the requirements of the capital, which is growing bigger all the time, demand centralisation of decision-making. The centralisation of state power is in part a reflection of this inner logic inherent in the capitalist development. The consequent erosion of the rights of the states or denial of autonomy to them is not simply a matter of will of this or that leader or this or that party in a simple sense; there are deeper forces working. This is a trend discernible all over the world. The history of the evolution of the federation in USA or Canada clearly shows this. Hence the issue of state autonomy and state rights is more than a question of simple choice between federal and unitary preferences on only a constitutional level, in spite of the fact that the constitutional division of power is very important. The trend towards the centralisation of power is inherent but how it works out in specific circumstances in different countries is dependent on the configuration of political forces.

THE INDIAN CASE

We are not looking at the global trends but only at the case of India. Let us look at Indian politics by breaking it into three landmark phases:

- the uninterrupted rule of the Congress party from 1947 to 1977,
- the rule of the Janata Party from 1977-1979, the return of the Congress in 1980, and
- the continuing era of coalition politics since 1996.

The Phase of Congress Hegemony: 1947-1977   Book Q.2

In India in particular, the process of political centralisation was facilitated by the more or less uninterrupted rule of the Congress party for the first 30 years both at the centre and in most of the states and was necessitated by the challenges to the hegemony of the Congress rule. The Congress moves were the attempts of an insecure leadership in the face of the mounting crisis of the capitalist path of development. In fact, due to the failures of the economy to even mitigate the hardships of the people, solving the basic problems apart, the Indian political system has been in a state of semi-permanent crisis. The political dominance of the Congress and its hegemony over state power not only helped it to contain by repression or manipulations the recurrent political crises but also aggravated, by the very logic of the situation, the tendency towards the centralisation and concentration of political power.

in spite of important discontinuities, the great similarities between the periods 1967-1969 and 1977-1979 with respect to the fortunes of the political parties as well as to the heightened articulation of the demand for state autonomy. Both these periods witnessed the decline of the Congress Party and the emergence of the regional political parties and formations to political prominence. In both the situations, apart from one or two states, the regional or regionally-based parties that gained at the cost of the Congress party were the ruling class regional parties. Similarly, the parties which formed governments in different states on both these occasions, were providing opposition to the Congress party both at the centre and in the states within a framework of similar policy preferences, e.g., Akalis in Punjab, the Bharatiya Kranti Dal in Uttar Pradesh, the Dravida Munnetra Kazhagam in Tamil Nadu, etc.

The Janata Phase: 1977-1979   Book Q.2

The nature of the Janata Party in power at the centre was unlike any other party. It was a conglomerate of many opposition parties and its birth was an outcome of a rapid coming together of disparate opposition groups ranging from Jan Sangh to the Socialists and the breakaway group of the Congress party under Jagjivan Ram. Their interests and programmes were naturally very different. An extraordinary situation, the need to defeat the emergency regime of Indira Gandhi, brought them together. These parties became factions within the newly formed Janata Party and continued to represent their earlier interests and programmes; Jana Sangh of the commercial petty-bourgeoisie or feudal landlords in certain regions, the BLD/BKD/Lok Dal of landlords and kulaks in three or four states of northern India.

Such a conglomeration ruled at the centre but its different constituents were in power in different States in uneasy alliances with other constituents. In the absence of a viable compromise formula, their different social bases and mass support forced them to horse-trade within the Janata Party to so tilt the policies that their mass supports could be sustained. It also happened that the Janata party was much more dependent for its rule on the various regional parties than was the Congress except for a brief while during 1969-1971. The absence of internal cohesion as well of intra-party consensus on vital issues made it difficult for it to impose its will or to effectively protect or guide the ruling classes.

This division was not, from an ideological point of view, fundamentally different from what existed earlier. But there was a very significant fact: the support for the ruling class parties became, and was becoming, more and more atomised and relatively evenly spread whereas earlier it was concentrated around one party, the Congress party. Moreover, the left forces, especially the CPI(M), became relatively much more powerful than ever before without, however, having become decisive in the all-India context.

> ### The Phase of Coalition Politics   Book Q.3

At the present moment, there is no movement for state autonomy like earlier even though the struggle to get more financial resources for the state continues. In the 1990 a visible change came in the correlation of forces active in the Indian politics. Conventionally speaking, it is, on the European example, a coalitional pattern. But given the multi-ethnic specificity of India, it is, on a deeper analysis, more than a coalition. It is much more a co-governance of the country by the nation and the regions which make up the nation. What constitutes the Centre at the level of the nation-state is made up as much of those who speak on behalf of and claim to represent the nation as much as those who do so for the various regions. In fact, this configuration has been a result of a long contestation, going back to the early years of Independence, between various forces as to how and by whom will the "nation" be represented; what will be the cultural identity marks of the nation(-

state). The result is a slow process towards congealing of the respective claims of the diverse forces representing the nation-state and the different regional states. One cannot do without the other. I am calling it a co-governance in that sense. Now the sense of this will become clear if we compare it with an earlier period in the history of governance in India.

It is quite clear from the above that this period in the 1990s has been marked by a pronounced ascendance of regional parties in a somewhat enduring manner. In the short term (now there is no long term trend that can be analytically discerned in Indian politics), there seem to be no chance of this trend being reversed. But what informs the ascendance of the regional parties is the absence of any overt conflicts or clashes between the centre and the state in India however much of differences of opinions can be shown to exist on any number of issues. What seems to be happening between the centre and state in terms of differences of opinion are in the nature of symbiotic contests. This trend crystallised during the period of the two United Front ministries in 1996-97. Even the BJP with its chauvinistic nationalism and rabid communalism and centralising ideology has been forced to accept the pattern and pay lip service to the code of behaviour entailed within these patterns. Barring a region here and there on the borders, the national unity of India seems to be acquiring deeper roots. It will be an effort of the argument here to look for reasons and some causal chains in the making of this phenomenon.

17.2: IGNOU Book Exercise – Solved

1) Identify the features of autonomy movements.

Answer by India Ebook: Read the 1 Shot Concept Above.

2) Compare the nature of autonomy movements between the phases of Congress hegemony and the Janata rule.

Answer by India Ebook: Read the 1 Shot Concept Above.

3) Comment on the autonomy movements during the era of coalition politics.

Answer by India Ebook: Read the 1 Shot Concept Above.

17.3: IGNOU Past 6 Attempts Question – Solved

June 2019: Write short note: (a) Autonomy Movements

Answer by India Ebook: Same as Q.1 Above.